CIVIL WARS IN AFRICA

CIVIL WARS IN AFRICA

William Mark Habeeb

Mason Crest Publishers

Philadelphia

Frontispiece: A Congolese refugee sits in front of his makeshift home, circa 2004.

Produced by OTTN Publishing, Stockton, New Jersey

Mason Crest Publishers
370 Reed Road
Broomall, PA 19008
www.masoncrest.com

First printing

1 3 5 7 9 8 6 4 2

Library of Congress Cataloging-in-Publication Data

  Habeeb, William Mark, 1955-
  Civil wars in Africa / William Mark Habeeb.
      v. cm. — (Africa, progress and problems)
  Includes bibliographical references and index.
  ISBN-13: 978-1-59084-955-2
  ISBN-10: 1-59084-955-8
  1. Civil war—Africa. 2. Africa—Social conditions—1960- 3. Africa—Politics and government—1960- I.
Title. II. Series.
  DT30.5.H32 2006
  303.6'4096—dc22
                        2006010768

TABLE OF CONTENTS

AFRICA: PROGRESS & PROBLEMS

THE PROMISE OF TODAY'S AFRICA

by Robert I. Rotberg

oday's Africa is a mosaic of effective democracy and desperate despotism, immense wealth and abysmal poverty, conscious modernity and mired traditionalism, bitter conflict and vast arenas of peace, and enormous promise and abiding failure. Generalizations are more difficult to apply to Africa or Africans than elsewhere. The continent, especially the sub-Saharan two-thirds of its immense landmass, presents enormous physical, political, and human variety. From snow-capped peaks to intricate patches of remaining jungle, from desolate deserts to the greatest rivers, and from the highest coastal sand dunes anywhere to teeming urban conglomerations, Africa must be appreciated from myriad perspectives. Likewise, its peoples come in every shape and size, govern themselves in several complicated manners, worship a host of indigenous and imported gods, and speak thousands of original and five or six derivative common languages. To know Africa is to know nuance and complexity.

There are 53 nation-states that belong to the African Union, 48 of which are situated within the sub-Saharan mainland or on its offshore islands. No other continent has so many countries, political divisions, or members of the General Assembly of the United Nations. No other continent encompasses so many

distinctively different peoples or spans such geographical disparity. On no other continent have so many innocent civilians lost their lives in intractable civil wars—12 million since 1991 in such places as Algeria, Angola, the Congo, Côte d'Ivoire, Liberia, Sierra Leone, and the Sudan. No other continent has so many disparate natural resources (from cadmium, cobalt, and copper to petroleum and zinc) and so little to show for their frenzied exploitation. No other continent has proportionally so many people subsisting (or trying to) on less than $1 a day. But then no other continent has been so beset by HIV/AIDS (30 percent of all adults in southern Africa), by tuberculosis, by malaria (prevalent almost everywhere), and by less well-known scourges such as schistosomiasis (liver fluke), several kinds of filariasis, river blindness, trachoma, and trypanosomiasis (sleeping sickness).

Africa is the most Christian continent. It has more Muslims than the Middle East. Apostolic and Pentecostal churches are immensely powerful. So are Sufi brotherhoods. Yet traditional African religions are still influential. So is a belief in spirits and witches (even among Christians and Muslims), in faith healing and in alternative medicine. Polygamy remains popular. So does the practice of female circumcision and other long-standing cultural preferences. Africa cannot be well understood without appreciating how village life still permeates the great cities and how urban pursuits engulf villages. Half if not more of its peoples live in towns and cities; no longer can Africa be considered predominantly rural, agricultural, or wild.

Political leaders must cater to both worlds, old and new. They and their followers must join the globalized, Internet-penetrated world even as they remain rooted appropriately in past modes of behavior, obedient to dictates of family, lineage, tribe, and ethnicity. This duality often results in democracy or at

least partially participatory democracy. Equally often it develops into autocracy. Botswana and Mauritius have enduring democratic governments. In Benin, Ghana, Kenya, Lesotho, Malawi, Mali, Mozambique, Namibia, Nigeria, Senegal, South Africa, Tanzania, and Zambia fully democratic pursuits are relatively recent and not yet sustainably implanted. Algeria, Cameroon, Chad, the Central African Republic, Egypt, the Sudan, and Tunisia are authoritarian entities run by strongmen. Zimbabweans and Equatorial Guineans suffer from even more venal rule. Swazis and Moroccans are subject to the real whims of monarchs. Within even this vast sweep of political practice there are still more distinctions. The partial democracies represent a spectrum. So does the manner in which authority is wielded by kings, by generals, and by long-entrenched civilian autocrats.

The democratic countries are by and large better developed and more rapidly growing economically than those ruled by strongmen. In Africa there is an association between the pursuit of good governance and beneficial economic performance. Likewise, the natural resource wealth curse that has afflicted mineral-rich countries such as the Congo and Nigeria has had the opposite effect in well-governed places like Botswana. Nation-states open to global trade have done better than those with closed economies. So have those countries with prudent managements, sensible fiscal arrangements, and modest deficits. Overall, however, the bulk of African countries have suffered in terms of reduced economic growth from the sheer fact of being tropical, beset by disease in an enervating climate

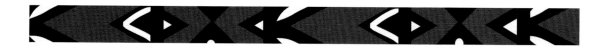

where there is an average of one trained physician to every 13,000 persons. Many lose growth prospects, too, because of the absence of navigable rivers, the paucity of ocean and river ports, barely maintained roads, and few and narrow railroads. Moreover, 15 of Africa's countries are landlocked, without comfortable access to relatively inexpensive waterborne transport. Hence, imports and exports for much of Africa are more expensive than elsewhere as they move over formidable distances. Africa is the most underdeveloped continent because of geographical and health constraints that have not yet been overcome, because of ill-considered policies, because of the sheer number of separate nation-states (a colonial legacy), and because of poor governance.

Africa's promise is immense, and far more exciting than its achievements have been since a wave of nationalism and independence in the 1960s liberated nearly every section of the continent. Thus, the next several decades of the 21st century are ones of promise for Africa. The challenges are clear: to alleviate grinding poverty and deliver greater real economic goods to larger proportions of people in each country, and across all 53 countries; to deliver more of the benefits of good governance to more of Africa's peoples; to end the destructive killing fields that run rampant across so much of Africa; to improve educational training and health services; and to roll back the scourges of HIV/AIDS, tuberculosis, and malaria. Every challenge represents an opportunity with concerted and bountiful Western assistance to transform the lives of Africa's vulnerable and resourceful future generations.

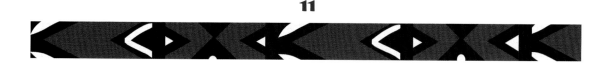

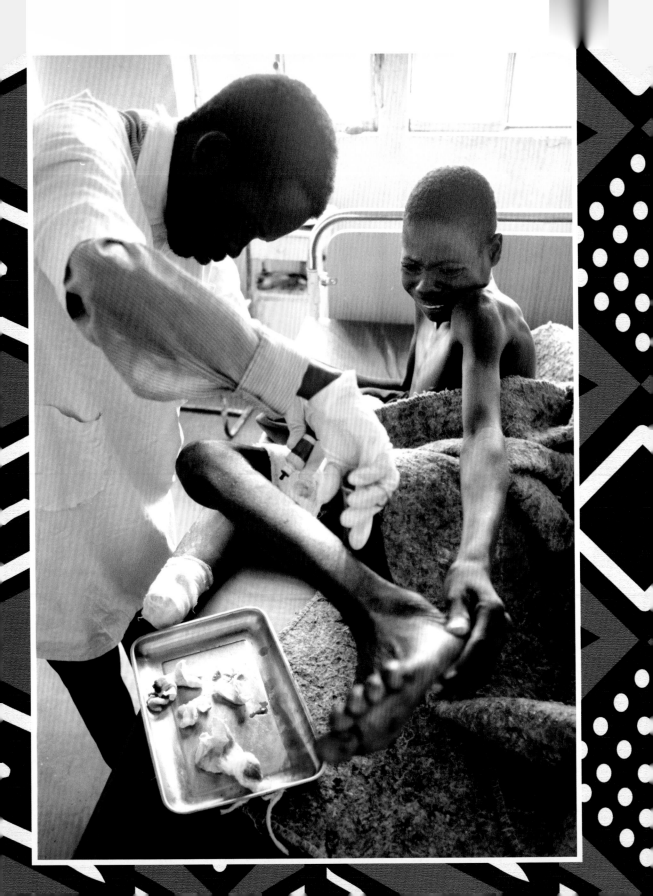

1 A CONTINENT TORN BY WAR

Africa is the world's most diverse continent. It is home to 885 million people, representing over 100 major ethnic groups. It contains vast reserves of natural resources, from oil and iron ore to gold and diamonds. More than 1,000 languages are spoken in Africa, and Africans practice every major world religion, along with dozens of ancient belief systems. Africa's history stretches back literally to the dawn of time: most anthropologists believe that the human race first appeared in Africa.

Modern Africa contains more than 50 countries, most of which became independent only after World War II, when the European colonial powers that had governed much of Africa since the 19th century withdrew. African countries share much in common in addition to their relative youth as nations. With only a few exceptions, each are ethnically diverse and home to multiple cultures, traditions, and languages. They are generally poor countries, despite the continent's rich resource base and the dynamic entrepreneurial traditions of many of its people.

Tragically, far too many African nations share something else in common: a history of bloody civil wars, ethnic violence, and secessionist uprisings. A civil war occurs when two or more groups within the same country struggle for control of state power. Since 1960, more than a dozen African countries have been devastated by civil war, several others have experienced the violent secession of a province or region, and many have been adversely affected by civil wars in neighboring countries.

Africa is certainly not the only area of the world to experience civil war. In recent decades, countries in the Balkans, Central America, and South Asia have suffered from violence that has torn societies apart. But on no other continent have civil wars been as widespread or as deadly as in Africa. In the year 2000, for example, 300,000 people throughout the world died as a result of conflict and war; over half of those deaths were in Africa. Today, it is estimated that between 20 and 25 percent of Africa's 885 million people are affected, either directly or indirectly, by ongoing civil wars.

THE HUMAN CONSEQUENCES OF CIVIL WAR

The toll in human lives lost in Africa's civil wars is staggering. For example, an ongoing civil war in the Democratic Republic of Congo (formerly Zaire) has claimed an estimated 4 million lives since 1998. More people have been killed in the Congolese civil war than in any conflict since World War II. The death tolls are lower, but no less tragic, in other conflicts. In Sudan, more than 2 million people died in the long-running civil war between the northern and southern areas of the country. Although Sudan's civil war officially ended in 2003 with a peace agreement, another conflict in that country's Darfur province had resulted in an additional 180,000 deaths by early 2006. In northern Uganda, 18 years of civil war between government troops and a rebel group known as the Lord's Resistance Army has claimed an estimated 100,000 lives. Angola's long civil war (1974–2002) led to at least 500,000 deaths. Between 1989 and 1996, civil war in the West African nation of Liberia killed 200,000 out of a population of only 2.5

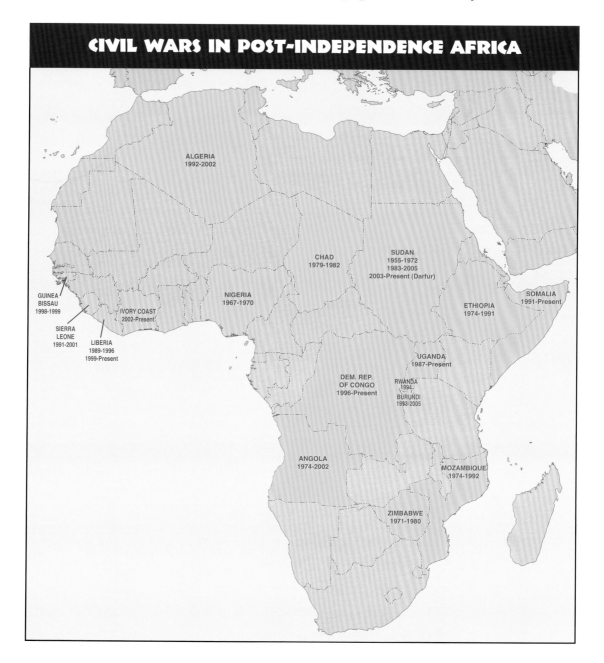

CIVIL WARS IN POST-INDEPENDENCE AFRICA

ALGERIA
1992-2002

CHAD
1979-1982

SUDAN
1955-1972
1983-2005
2003-Present (Darfur)

GUINEA
BISSAU
1998-1999

NIGERIA
1967-1970

SOMALIA
1991-Present

ETHIOPIA
1974-1991

IVORY COAST
2002-Present

SIERRA
LEONE
1991-2001

LIBERIA
1989-1996
1999-Present

UGANDA
1987-Present

DEM. REP.
OF CONGO
1996-Present

RWANDA
1994

BURUNDI
1993-2005

ANGOLA
1974-2002

MOZAMBIQUE
1974-1992

ZIMBABWE
1971-1980

million, and in the neighboring country of Sierra Leone, more than 20,000 people out of a total population of 5 million were killed in a civil war that ended in 2002. In Rwanda's bloody 1994 civil war, 800,000 people were killed in only three months of fighting, many in genocidal massacres.

For every person killed in Africa's civil wars, many others have been wounded, mutilated, or maimed for life, and millions have been made homeless refugees. Over 3 million Congolese now live in refugee camps in neighboring countries, and over 13 million have been "internally displaced" by war (meaning that they still live in Congo but not in their original home areas). Angola's civil war also generated around 3 million refugees. The civil war in southern Sudan left an estimated 4 million people uprooted, while an additional 2 million have been made refugees by the fighting in Darfur. The rebellion in Uganda has created 1.6 million refugees, while in Sierra Leone fully half of the population (2.5 million people) abandoned their homes due to fighting. In Rwanda, 1.5 million people fled to refugee camps in neighboring countries during the war, and another 1.5 million were internally displaced.

But death, injury, and homelessness are not the only consequences. Civil wars in Africa have almost always led to serious health crises. Because of their poverty, most African countries have inadequate health facilities to begin with; the chaos and destruction of civil war often has disrupted even the most minimal health services. Vaccination programs are terminated, millions of people no longer have access to health clinics, and doctors and nurses must spend an inordinate amount of time helping war casualties instead of performing their normal duties, such as inoculating children against common illnesses. Infectious diseases spread rapidly in areas where there is fighting and in squalid refugee camps. Poor sanitation, malnutrition, and lack of access to clean drinking water all contribute to the spread of illness.

Over the past four decades, millions of Africans have fled their homes because of civil wars or unrest in their countries. These children are waiting for meals in a refugee center in Angola.

Children, the elderly, and women are most vulnerable to sickness and starvation, and make up most of the deaths due to these causes. It is believed that over 70 percent of the 4 million deaths in Congo's bloody civil war have been due to disease, poor sanitation, and malnutrition.

Other social services, such as education and law enforcement, also suffer during civil conflict. Schools close (many are destroyed in the fighting), government offices are unable to pay their workers, and policemen either flee or get caught up in the conflict. The results include a poorly educated generation of children, unemployment, and an increase in crime.

As the social order breaks down, so do family structures. It is not unusual for a father and his older sons to be drafted into fighting (often by force), and for the mother to then flee to a far-away refugee camp with the family's young children. Family members lose contact with each other, and can only hope that they will be reunited one day. Millions of children have been made orphans by Africa's civil wars when both of their parents have been killed or died from disease; millions of others have been separated from one or both parents. The destruction of families—traditionally a source of strength and support for Africans—has been a cruel consequence of civil war.

CHILD SOLDIERS

Among the most offensive consequences of civil wars in Africa has been the widespread use of child soldiers. Children as young as eight years of age have been recruited into—or forced to join—militia groups and even official government armies. International organizations that work in Africa have estimated that at any given time, there are over 100,000 child soldiers actively participating in civil conflict; even the youngest among them carry weapons. Children who have been made orphans because of war and have nowhere else to turn for comfort are most vulnerable to becoming soldiers. Militia groups offer these children food, shelter, and protection. Some militia groups also offer money to child soldiers, enabling them to help support their families.

But children also have been forcibly torn from their families and pressed into joining militia groups. In exchange for food and shelter, the children must carry out any number of dangerous activities, such as laying land mines, manning roadblocks, and actually participating in battles. Because child soldiers generally obey whatever command they are given by the adult soldiers, they frequently are ordered to perform the most brutal acts of war, including the torture and murder of entire families.

The life of a child soldier is one of misery. Thousands have been killed or maimed in fighting. Many live a life of virtual slavery, subject to physical and sexual abuse. Children who try to flee these conditions risk execution; in any case, they

A child soldier of the Sudan People's Liberation Army rests at his unit's camp, circa 2000. Each year thousands of young Africans are forced to fight in civil wars.

usually have nowhere to go. Denied an education, most child soldiers are illiterate; even if they survive the war, they have virtually no useful life skills. Often those children who serve as soldiers are not welcomed back by their families and communities, who (with good reason) view them as dangerous and uncontrollable. Virtually all child soldiers suffer severe psychological trauma from their experiences, and without help risk becoming hardened criminals lacking the ability to form healthy human relationships.

The United Nations and a host of international organizations have attempted to focus the world's attention on the plight of child soldiers in Africa and elsewhere, but the practice of arming children continues, and there is no sign that this most tragic consequence of Africa's civil wars is abating.

THE ECONOMIC CONSEQUENCES OF CIVIL WAR

Africa is the world's poorest continent, and most African countries have struggled since independence to maintain economic growth at levels high enough to support growing populations. Famines and widespread starvation are not uncommon in Africa, and many African countries have survived largely on aid received from foreign governments and international organizations. Africa's civil wars have only worsened the continent's economic conditions and multiplied the economic challenges its people face. Africa is the only continent in the world whose people have grown poorer since 1980, and this sad fact is in large part due to civil war and violence.

Most African economies are based primarily on agriculture, but widespread fighting has forced farmers to abandon their land. On a personal level, this results in a loss of income for the farmer and his family, but when it occurs on a large scale the country faces an increased risk of food shortages and deadly famine. Fighting in rural areas causes mass migration to the continent's already overcrowded cities, straining urban infrastructure and causing high unemployment, crime, and epidemics of disease. Fighting in cities has the reverse effect: people flee into the countryside, leaving the cities empty ghost towns devoid of any significant economic activity.

Economies cannot grow without investment—public or private sector spending on new factories and stores, government services, and infrastructure. But when a civil war breaks out, investment in the nation grinds to a halt. After all, who would want to open a new business in a country wracked by violence, with an uncertain future? Those Africans who have significant amounts of money frequently take it out of the country—a phenomenon known as capital flight—instead of investing it in new projects. On a per capita basis, Africa suffers from a higher degree of capital flight than any other place in the world. Thanks to civil war and conflict, billions of dollars of African wealth is today deposited in bank accounts in Switzerland, France, or the United States, instead of being used to spur economic growth in African countries.

Money is not the only thing that leaves Africa when civil wars erupt. Often, the wealthier and better-educated members of society—those most likely to stimulate the economy or provide needed services—will flee to safer places. This phenomenon is commonly known as "brain drain."

Foreign investors also avoid African countries that are in the midst of civil war, thus denying African economies desperately needed funds for economic growth. In 2001, the entire African continent attracted only $17.7 billion in investment from foreign companies, according to the most recent data available from the International Monetary Fund. By comparison, during the same year foreign companies invested $67 billion in China and $24.7 billion in Mexico.

A boy stands outside of his destroyed home in the village of Dubie, Democratic Republic of the Congo. The destruction caused by civil wars makes it unlikely that foreign businesses will invest in African countries. This in turn leads to a lower standard of living and economic disparity that makes unrest and revolution more likely.

Africa receives billions of dollars every year in foreign aid from governments and international organizations. In 2003, according to the Organisation for Economic Cooperation and Development (OECD), Africa received just over $15 billion in aid from wealthier nations, more than any other region of the world. Some of this money has been spent on projects that help promote employment, education, health care, and economic growth. But during times of civil war, much of the foreign aid African countries receive is used to equip government armies to fight rebel groups, or to meet emergency needs, such as the provision of health care, refugee relocation, food, and water. While these critical needs must be met in times of war, they divert resources that could have been used for economic growth.

Moreover, some analysts have estimated that Africa's civil wars cost its people around $15 billion every year in destruction and lost income—essentially equal to the amount of foreign aid the continent receives.

Africa's civil wars tend to spill over into neighboring countries, thus inflicting them with many of the same humanitarian and economic problems. For example, when a civil war broke out in Liberia, its West African neighbor Guinea was forced to house hundreds of thousands of Liberian refugees fleeing from the fighting. These refugees not only created an economic burden for Guinea, but their presence also threatened the country's own political and social stability.

This Red Cross booth was set up in a camp for Liberian refugees, to help families reunite after being separated by the conflict in that country. When civil wars occur, foreign aid often must be diverted to help the victims. This means it cannot be used on economic development projects, which would help citizens escape the crushing poverty that in most cases contributed to the outbreak of conflict.

THE COST TO THE WORLD

There are many reasons the world should be concerned about civil wars that occur in African nations. From a humanitarian perspective, the death and destruction caused by African civil wars is unacceptable. The world simply cannot look the other way while an entire continent descends further into economic and human misery. The innocent victims of war—refugees, children, persecuted ethnic groups—are especially deserving of concern and attention.

From an economic perspective, there also are reasons to be concerned about conflict in Africa. With a market of nearly 900 million people and a wealth of natural resources, Africa has the potential to play a dynamic role in worldwide economic growth and prosperity. But Africa's potential cannot be met while so many of its nations are mired in or threatened by civil conflict. Africa's people cannot acquire the education and skills they need to compete economically in the 21st century if their nations are being torn apart by violence and war. Africa needs billions of dollars in investment, and the continent is filled with potentially profitable investment opportunities. But investors' greatest fear is instability and violence. As long as Africa has a reputation for civil war and conflict, investors will look elsewhere, thus leaving Africa's great economic potential largely unfulfilled.

Finally, civil war and violence in Africa pose a political and security risk to the entire world. African nations that have descended into civil war become lawless countries, where terrorist organizations, drug gangs, and common criminals operate freely. Governments are unable to secure their borders, and often have control over very little beyond the capital city. Public services—such as schools, hospitals, and power or utility companies—grind to a halt. Banks close or go out of business, and normal trade and commercial relationships fall apart. People often survive on barter or petty crime. National police and security forces disintegrate, or their members join militia armies. Judicial systems collapse, and no one is held accountable for even the worst of crimes. Political scientists have come up with a term—"failed states"—to describe this situation.

In the early years of the 21st century, the greatest threats to world peace have come from international terrorist groups like Osama bin Laden's al-Qaeda organization. These groups thrive within failed states—as al-Qaeda did in Afghanistan between 1996 and 2001—because there is no coherent, legitimate government force willing or able to confront them. Moreover, failed states serve as the best recruiting ground for terrorist groups. In the face of widespread misery and poverty, these groups offer individuals protection and support. It is therefore in the world's interest that African countries succeed in forming peaceful, stable societies.

THE CAUSES OF CIVIL WARS

At the most basic level, civil wars are about power. When one group within a country feels marginalized, it may seek power for itself though an armed insurrection against the party or group that controls the country. However, it is often difficult to point to a single factor that causes a civil war to begin. Many things contribute to the outbreak of civil war, including ethnic, cultural, and religious differences; political secessionist movements; and ideological disagreements. Frequently, economic disparity and bad government are at the root of conflict, creating the conditions in which instability and civil wars occur. Many rebellions begin as a backlash against governmental corruption or greed.

Each one of the factors mentioned above has played a role in causing or prolonging civil wars in Africa. In this regard, Africa is no different from the rest of the world. Civil wars are by no

Armed members of a rebel group ride through the Darfur region of western Sudan. The conflict between the government-supported Janjaweed militia and non-Arab rebels in the region began in early 2003; to date, more than 150,000 people have been killed and nearly 2 million have been forced from their homes.

means limited to Africa; conflicts are currently ongoing in Russia's Chechnya province, in Mexico's state of Chiapas, in the Mindanao region of the Philippines, in Northern Ireland, and in Sri Lanka. Wherever civil wars occur, there are high civilian casualty rates and horrific atrocities. But the fact remains that over the past 50 years, more civil wars have occurred in Africa than on any other continent.

To understand why Africa seems more susceptible to civil wars, careful analysis of both past and current conditions in the continent is required. To be sure, much of the responsibility for civil conflicts can be attributed to Africa's tradition of poor governments. The excesses of leaders like Mohammad Siad Barre of Somalia, Mobutu Sese Seko of Zaire/Congo, and Robert Mugabe of Zimbabwe contribute to the extreme poverty of their country's people; there is certainly a significant connection between this crushing poverty and civil war. In addition, throughout history outside powers have provoked and sustained civil wars in Africa. To understand Africa's civil wars, a person must first understand the historical context in which many African countries and their governmental systems were formed, and then look at the other important factors that have contributed to the continent's sad history of violence and conflict.

THE IMPACT OF COLONIALISM ON AFRICA

(Opposite) A session of the 1884–85 Berlin Conference, at which Europeans redrew the boundaries of Africa and divided the continent amongst themselves. Representatives of the African peoples were not invited to attend.

Today, many Africans believe that the seeds of their continent's problems were planted during the late 19th and early 20th centuries. Between 1870 and 1913, European powers carved up Africa into spheres of influence, and established colonies to rule and exploit. These European states were following a policy known as colonialism, which occurs when a nation extends its sovereignty over territory and people outside its own borders. Often, the purpose of colonialism is to enrich the mother country by controlling trade with the colony and exploiting its natural and human resources.

Europeans had long been involved in Africa. Portugal, Britain, France, and other countries all possessed colonies along the coasts. However, much of the continent remained free of foreign control until the late 19th century, when the major European powers began to view Africa as an extension of their struggles for dominance in Europe. Thus began a scramble to colonize the interior of the continent. France established colonies in North and West Africa, while Britain dominated Egypt, Sudan, southern Africa, and East Africa. The Horn of Africa—the name given to the northeastern part of the continent just below Egypt and Sudan—was divided among the British, French, and Italians. The Portuguese maintained control over large coastal areas of southwestern and southeastern Africa, as well as a small colony in West Africa (today the country of Guinea Bissau). The Belgians established a colony in what is today the Congo, while Germany and Spain also claimed areas of the continent.

In order to avoid confrontations and prevent potential conflict over Africa, the European powers met in Berlin during 1884–85 to formally divide the continent among themselves. The Berlin Conference, as it came to be known, drew new political boundaries in Africa that reflected the interests and demands of the

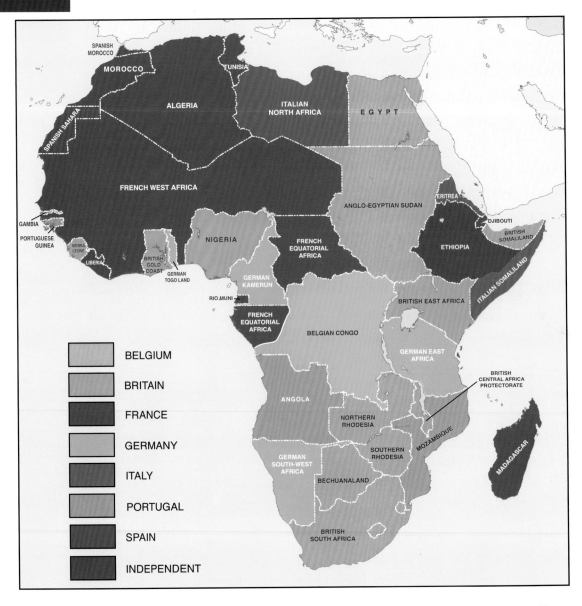

This map of Africa shows how the continent was divided up among European countries. Pictured here are the colonial boundaries in 1913, shortly before the outbreak of the First World War.

colonial powers. But these boundaries did not take into account where various ethnic groups lived, or the traditional trade and social relationships among Africa's peoples. Thus, most of these colonies were home to multiple ethnic groups—often groups that had traditionally been rivals or enemies, spoke different languages, and had no experience living together peacefully. In some cases, members of a large ethnic group found themselves scattered among several new countries. The Malinke people, for example, found themselves living in the West African colonies that would eventually become the states of Gambia, Guinea, Guinea Bissau, Mali, Mauritania, and Senegal. The Tuareg people were spread among the colonies that would become Niger, Nigeria, Burkina Faso, Senegal, and Mali. The Maasai people could be found in both German East Africa (modern-day Tanzania) and British East Africa (Kenya). No representatives of African peoples were invited to the conference or played any role in drawing up their continent's new boundaries. These would become the borders of African states when the colonial powers withdrew from Africa, granting independence to former colonies during the 1960s and 1970s.

COLONIAL EXPLOITATION OF AFRICA

During the scramble for Africa, some European leaders publicly stated that their purpose for establishing colonies was to provide the benefits of Western civilization to the indigenous peoples. It became commonplace to speak of the "white man's burden"—a duty that Europeans felt to spread their "superior" culture to the "savages" of Africa.

In practice, however, the colonial powers did little to help develop a sense of nationhood among the various peoples living under their control. On the contrary, colonial administrators exacerbated—and sometimes even created—tensions among ethnic groups in order to keep the population divided and thus easier to control. The last thing the colonial rulers wanted was for the African population to become unified, because then it might seek self-government.

The European powers were interested in Africa primarily because of the continent's wealth of natural resources. They set up companies—controlled, of course, by agents of the colonial power—to extract these resources and export them. Colonial administrators were primarily interested in exploiting the wealth and resources of their colony. They devoted little more than lip service to the important task of establishing the social and political infrastructure needed for the colony to one day become independent.

Colonial administrators also were not concerned with building strong, diverse economies that would sustain the colony once it became independent. In fact, in many cases their actions disrupted and undermined existing institutions and economic traditions. For example, in Côte d'Ivoire, the French established huge plantations to grow coffee, sugar, and cocoa—products that French consumers desired—forcing Ivorian farmers to abandon traditional food crops. In Kenya, which was a British colony

A Kenyan woman walks with her children on a British coffee plantation during the 1930s. The European powers exploited the resources of their African colonies to enrich and strengthen their own empires.

from 1895 until 1963, the most fertile agricultural land was reserved for white British settlers. In Angola, Portuguese colonists established coffee, cotton, and sugar cane plantations during the early 20th century. Thousands of Portuguese settlers moved to Angola to run the plantations and farms, with local Africans providing the labor—often under conditions of virtual slavery.

Conditions were even worse in Belgian Congo, which Belgium's King Leopold established as a personal possession that he ruled with a mercenary army. Most of the working-age population of the colony was forced to work in mines and on rubber plantations. Between 4 and 8 million Congolese were killed in massacres, and millions of others died of starvation and disease. But King Leopold became one of Europe's wealthiest men as a result of his economic exploitation of Congo.

Some people have argued that colonial rule benefits the colonized, because the ruling nation develops the economic infrastructure and political traditions within the country that are necessary for modernization and democracy. Former colonies like the United States, Canada, Australia, and Singapore are sometimes cited as examples of postcolonial success. However, these examples are not typical—few former colonies have achieved a similar level of success.

Other modern scholars believe that colonialism stifles, rather than encourages, positive economic development within

At the Berlin Conference, King Leopold II of Belgium gained control of a vast area of central Africa called the Congo Free State. Leopold ruled this territory as a personal domain rather than a Belgian colony. To maximize the extraction of rubber, ivory, and other valuable resources, Leopold's colonial managers enslaved, tortured, and murdered millions of Congolese.

colonies. In 1950, the Argentine economist Raul Prebisch theorized that when colonies send raw materials (such as timber, iron ore, foodstuffs, cotton, oil, and other products) to the mother country, they are actually transferring their wealth. The colonizer benefits from the import of these goods, as well as from trade in finished goods that are exported to its colony. Therefore, Prebisch found, the relationship inhibits economic growth in the colony. For this reason, he wrote, developing countries should diversify their economies and lessen dependence on primary commodity exports by developing their manufacturing industry. Other critics of colonialism, such as Frantz Fanon and Aimé Césaire, have argued that colonial policies caused political, psychological, and moral damage to the indigenous people.

It is certainly true that native residents of the African colonies enjoyed few rights. The colonial governments established by the European powers were highly centralized and authoritarian, often led by military figures. The colonial powers had little interest in promoting democracy, individual liberties, or human rights—particularly when these things conflicted with their exploitation of the colony's resources. Africans generally had no legal or political way to protest against the actions of colonial authorities. Colonial military and police forces were employed to suppress dissent and ensure control over both the land and the people. Opposition leaders were arrested, and local political movements that opposed colonial rule were outlawed.

RESISTANCE AND DECOLONIZATION

After the First World War, many new states were created from the territories of once-powerful empires, such as the Austro-Hungarian and Ottoman empires. The League of Nations, an international body established in the 1919 Treaty of Versailles, provided a mechanism for the transition of colonies

The Greatest Moment in History

Exclusive Photographs by HELEN JOHNS KIRTLAND and LUCIAN SWIFT KIRTLAND, Leslie's Staff Correspondents

The signing of the Peace Treaty at Versailles on June 28th formally ended the greatest war in the history of the world, and as the German delegates attached their signatures the thoughts of many turned back to the days of 1871 when Bismarck imposed his stern conditions on the French delegates in the same hall.

First Two Pages of Peace Treaty Signatures

The Treaty of Versailles (1919), which ended the First World War, established a system of mandates by which European powers were supposed to prepare their colonies for independence. However, African colonies did not gain their freedom until after the end of World War II, when countries like Britain and France could no longer afford to maintain their colonial empires.

to independence. Article 22 of the League's Covenant established a system of mandates, by which "those colonies . . . inhabited by peoples not yet able to stand by themselves under the strenuous conditions of the modern world" would be groomed for self-government under the guidance of developed nations. In reality, the mandate system was a way that the victorious Allied powers (particularly Britain and France) could gain control over the former colonies of the defeated Central powers (Germany, Austria-Hungary, and the Ottoman empire).

Between 1920 and the start of World War II in 1939, movements developed in some parts of Africa to resist colonialism. These resistance movements grew especially strong after World War II ended in 1945. The European nations, devastated economically by the Second World War, found they could no longer afford to maintain their colonial empires. They began to work with nationalist leaders in Africa and elsewhere to plan the transition to independence for their colonies.

The political process of transitioning a nation-state from colonial status to self-government is sometimes called decolonization. Decolonization usually involves a combination of insurrection—including either violent or nonviolent methods—by the indigenous people against the colonial authority, and peaceful negotiation between colonial and nationalist leaders.

In countries like Ghana and Kenya, internal pressure led to the relatively peaceful transfer of power in 1957 and 1963, respectively. In other places, the Europeans attempted to hold onto their colonies, and conflicts with the indigenous nationalists evolved into full-scale wars of independence. Algerians, for example, fought a long and extremely bloody war against the French from 1954 to 1962, while both Angola and Mozambique were wracked by lengthy wars of independence against the Portuguese.

AN UNFORTUNATE BEGINNING

By the early 1970s, nearly all of Africa's countries had gained their independence. However, this did not mark the end of colonial-era problems. On the contrary, the newly independent African states came into being with serious handicaps that their new governments lacked the capabilities and resources to quickly or easily overcome.

One of these problems was the fractured social nature of the former colonies. European rule had served to unite different factions as they struggled for independence. Once they achieved their freedom, the Africans often splintered into ethnic, religious, class, or regional factions. Rather than working together to build a unified country, in many cases the various groups sought to dominate and control rivals within the country.

In addition, some experts believe that the violent rebellions required to bring about independence helped create the impression among Africans that the only way to change a government was through force of arms. This may have influenced the way African governments transferred power. During the early post-independence years, Africa was plagued by military coups d'etat, in which the ruling government was overthrown by military force. Between 1960 and 1970, there were at least 21 military coups in Africa in which a country's leader was either deposed or killed and a new leader installed. Several countries—such as Nigeria, Congo, and Algeria—suffered multiple coups during this decade. By 1975, nearly half of all African states were ruled by a military government.

Bad governance has been a problem in Africa for decades, and some scholars consider this another legacy of colonialism. Once African countries gained independence, their new governments often mirrored the structure of the colonial governments, for this was the only model of government they knew. Thus, the newly independent African states tended to be led by authoritarian figures who put up with little or no opposition, and who viewed their country's wealth as something to be exploited for personal gain. Control of the military was the key to power, just as the colonial rulers had also maintained power through the use of force. Men like Mobutu Sese Seko of Zaire (Congo), Siad Barre in Somalia, Idi Amin in Uganda, Sekou Toure in Guinea, and Jean-Bedel Bokassa in the Central African Republic ruled their countries as ruthless dictators.

Not all of Africa's early leaders fit this pattern. Seretse Khama of Botswana and Seewoosagur Ramgoolam of Mauritius were two dynamic and charismatic leaders who established a democratic tradition for their young nations. It is perhaps no coincidence that their countries are among the most prosperous in Africa, and have avoided serious unrest or civil war.

Sir Seretse Khama (1921–1980) helped guide Botswana to independence in 1966 and served as the country's first president. His policies helped Botswana develop peacefully; today, the country is among Africa's most prosperous nations. Unfortunately, most African rulers have not matched the standard of leadership set by Seretse Khama.

CONCLUSION

Scholars have mixed views about colonization's impact on Africa. Some believe that decolonization occurred too quickly in Africa, and that this resulted in the creation of unstable regimes in the newly independent countries. Others argue that this instability is largely the result of colonial-era problems, such as the arbitrary borders established by the Europeans, the dearth of education and training, and economic issues. What most people agree upon, however, is that although colonial policies may have created the conditions for some of Africa's problems, the despots who have plagued African nations for the past five decades deserve most of the blame for the continent's violent history of civil wars.

BAD GOVERNMENT AND ECONOMIC MISMANAGEMENT

pon achieving independence, many African countries fell into a similar pattern. Their governments came under the control of an individual—often the nationalist leader of the country's anticolonial movement—who quickly assumed the same all-powerful role as the former colonial rulers. These leaders used their country's armed forces to maintain order and to suppress opposition. Their goal became staying in power, rather than building prosperous societies with strong governmental institutions and the rule of law. These leaders ruled with absolute authority over their state, prohibiting opposition political parties or an independent judicial system.

But corrupt governments are often inefficient and dysfunctional. In most such countries, government employees are poorly trained; police and military forces place themselves above the law; and the courts have no real authority or independence. As societies became less democratic and the rule of law is weakened, average citizens have little or no opportunity to express frustration and grievances, or to bring about change peacefully.

CASE STUDY: SIERRA LEONE

Sierra Leone, a small country in western Africa, provides an example of how bad governance can lead a country into civil war. When Sierra Leone became independent in 1961, the country had inherited a good educational system from the British. The country had other advantages as well, including abundant natural resources, good agricultural land, and a democratically elected government. But after Siaka Stevens became Sierra Leone's prime minister in 1968, he gradually took complete control of the country. Stevens appointed friends and political allies to key government positions, and government corruption became widespread. Stevens and his cronies also diverted millions of dollars from diamond mining and other industries to their personal bank accounts, weakening the economy and plunging most residents of Sierra Leone into desperate poverty.

To stay in power, Stevens became an authoritarian leader, cracking down on political enemies. Under a new constitution that he engineered in 1978, Stevens's All Peoples' Congress (APC) became the only legitimate political party; all opposition parties were banned. When elections did not turn out the way the government wished, they were canceled or invalidated.

In authoritarian states, a change of power usually only occurs when the leader dies or through a successful coup d'etat. Often, these coups

are staged by the military, and a high-ranking officer assumes the leadership position. Stevens avoided both fates. His state police thwarted several attempted coups, and in 1985 he retired, turning over power to his chosen successor, Joseph Saidu Momoh. By the time Stevens stepped down, Sierra Leone's economy was barely functioning, and the country's people were among the world's poorest.

Although Stevens died three years before a civil war broke out in Sierra Leone, the corrupt system he had established and nurtured was a major cause of the violence. Many poor Sierra Leoneans resented the corruption of APC party leaders, and began to support a guerilla army called the Revolutionary United Front (RUF). The RUF promised to provide free education and health care, and to more equitably distribute the wealth from the country's profitable diamond mining industry. The RUF was supported by Libya, which at that time was seeking to create a network of friendly allies throughout Africa, as well as by a rebel group in neighboring Liberia headed by Charles Taylor.

The country's economic problems and the RUF's successes in eastern Sierra Leone led the military to overthrow the Momoh regime in 1992. However, the military government that replaced Momoh, the National Provisional Ruling Council (NPRC), proved to be similarly ineffectual at ending the RUF uprising.

The war in Sierra Leone was particularly brutal, as soldiers on both sides terrorized the country for more than a decade. The RUF became infamous for its policy of amputating the hands, arms, or legs of civilians in order to keep them from fighting for the government. After the RUF gained control of Sierra Leone's diamond mines, it used the proceeds to pay its troops and buy weapons. Among civilians, disease and starvation were common.

In 1999, the United Nations intervened in the civil war, sending a multinational peacekeeping force to regain order. Eventually the RUF was disarmed, its leader arrested as a war

Twelve-year-old Mamusu Koroma sits in a school for amputees at a refugee camp in Sierra Leone, circa 2001. Two years earlier, Mamusu was captured by RUF troops in Freetown. The soldiers raped the young girl repeatedly, then hacked off her right arm.

criminal, and a system for democratic elections was established. Eleven years of civil war had resulted in more than 20,000 people dead and tens of thousands maimed or homeless. It also left a poor country even poorer.

A COMMON PROBLEM IN AFRICA

Unfortunately, over the years this situation has occurred in several African countries. Numerous African strongmen—including Mohammad Siad Barre in Somalia, Samuel K. Doe in Liberia, Idi Amin in Uganda, Sekou Toure in Guinea, and Robert Mugabe in Zimbabwe—have exploited their nation's wealth, creating deep grievances in the process. One of Africa's worst leaders was Mobutu Sese Seko, who ruled Zaire from 1965 until

As president of Zaire/Congo for 30 years, Mobutu Sese Seko (1930–1997) used his country's resources to enrich himself and his family, while millions of citizens starved. Mobutu's corruption and heavy-handed repression of dissent caused Congo to collapse into civil war.

1997. Mobutu diverted billions of dollars from the sale of Zaire's natural resources (largely copper and diamonds) into his personal bank accounts, becoming one of the wealthiest men in the world while most of his countrymen lived in grinding poverty. Needless to say, his actions created deep resentment among the people of Zaire, and contributed to the civil war that erupted in that country after Mobutu's regime was overthrown in 1997.

POVERTY AND ECONOMIC ISSUES

Poverty is one of the most obvious results of bad governance, and there seems to be a clear connection between extreme poverty and civil war. Of the ten poorest African countries, when ranked in terms of gross domestic product per capita (that is, the total GDP divided by the country's population), five have experienced civil wars in the past 50 years. Of Africa's ten wealthiest countries, only one (Algeria) has suffered through civil war.

Economic disparity, in which some members of society control a disproportionate percentage of their country's total wealth, leads to grievances and resentment. Often, economic disparity occurs along ethnic or religious lines, as members of certain privileged groups benefit more from the country's wealth than do others. This is common in authoritarian societies, as despotic rulers tend to direct money and power to members of their own ethnic groups or even their families.

Extreme poverty may encourage people to identify more strongly with their ethnic group, clan, or family, especially when they are more likely to find sources of support there than from the government. This identification with an ethnic group may be strengthened if there is a feeling among its members that other ethnic groups are receiving greater economic benefits, or that the government is persecuting them.

When a nation's poor have little hope for the future, and hold grievances against those whom they perceive as better off, they will have little stake in the society. Consequently, they will have few qualms about committing violence against the government or other groups in the society. Charismatic rebel leaders actively recruit followers from among the underprivileged and impoverished. They try to exploit resentment by convincing unemployed young men that a violent overthrow of the current government will enhance their prospects for survival.

Civil wars cause greater poverty as the existing economic system is disturbed or destroyed. Even when a ruler is overthrown in a coup d'etat, the new leader usually redirects economic benefits to his own ethnic group or family, and the poverty and resentment continue. If this tragic cycle is not broken, a society may remain in a state of violent civil unrest for decades, with its people becoming more and more impoverished.

CONTROL OF NATURAL RESOURCES

Guerilla organizations often try to seize control of important economic assets—such as Sierra Leone's diamond mines—in order to have a means of paying recruits and financing their operations. For many of the poor and unemployed, joining a guerilla group is nothing more than a "job," and a means to earn income to support their families, even if they don't agree with the rebel organization's ideology or goals.

An important study conducted by the World Bank concluded that the existence of high-value natural resources that could be easily controlled and taken out of the country may be a significant factor in African civil wars. This occurred both in Sierra Leone and in neighboring Liberia. Each of these countries has rich reserves of gold and diamonds—two commodities that can easily be smuggled out of the country and sold illegally. Rebel groups in Sierra Leone and Liberia sought control over regions rich in these commodities, which they then sold to finance their

A supervisor holds diamonds at a government-controlled mine near Kenema, Sierra Leone. Diamonds mined legally by the government and illegally by the rebel RUF helped fund both sides of the civil war in Sierra Leone. The people forced to work the mines do not benefit from the wealth they find for government or rebel leaders—diamond panners like the ones pictured in the background are paid two cups of rice and about 25 cents a day.

rebellions. The RUF rebel group in Sierra Leone secured control of diamond mines before launching its rebellion; diamonds made the rebellion possible. Similarly, in Angola, the rebel UNITA group is believed to have sold billions of dollars worth of diamonds to finance its uprising against the government.

The risk of civil war is especially great in situations where valuable natural resources are located in a region of the country that is populated by one specific ethnic group who feels that it is not benefiting sufficiently from exploitation of the resource. Africa's secessionist civil wars have virtually always been related at least in part to a struggle over resources.

Soon after achieving independence in 1960, Congo (Zaire) faced a secessionist revolt in the province of Katanga, an area that contains vast copper mines and other mineral resources. The revolt was encouraged by foreign mining companies, who thought they could negotiate better business deals with the local population than with the central government. After three years of fighting—which also involved Belgian troops and UN peacekeepers—Katanga was reunited with Congo/Zaire. But periodic uprisings in the province continued to plague the central government for many years.

FAILED STATES

When authoritarian governments lose control of the state, as the Momoh regime did in Sierra Leone, the entire state may collapse. Eventually, the government may be unable to provide even the most basic services to its people. Scholars call this occurrence "state failure."

At the opposite end of the spectrum, a "successful" state can be defined as one that maintains a monopoly on the legitimate use of physical force within its borders. In the United States, for example, the government is solely responsible for maintaining civil order. Americans cannot take up arms against their government, even if they disagree with its actions. They can seek legal redress through the court system, or try to change government policies by voting for new leaders or through peaceful exercise of their First Amendment right to protest. But only agents of the government, such as the police, are permitted to use force to maintain order. Vigilante groups that use violence, even when attempting to uphold the law, are illegal in the United States.

When a state's monopoly on the use of force is broken—usually because of the emergence of armed militia groups, such as the RUF in Sierra Leone—the existence of the state itself becomes threatened. In some cases, the government loses control over parts of its territory. Such was the case in Sierra Leone and Liberia. In other cases, the state is rendered ineffective, with

Somali "politicians," some carrying semiautomatic rifles, gather in a stadium in the town of Baidoa, February 2006. Somalia is perhaps the best-known example of a failed state. Government control over the country collapsed in 1991; today there is no central government, and armed militias led by warlords control different parts of the country.

only nominal control over certain territories even though it is not directly challenged by an armed opposition group.

Failed states are characterized by economic stagnation and poverty; corruption and the inequitable exploitation of natural resource wealth; high crime; poor or nonexistent health and educational systems; and resentful populations who feel no connection or loyalty to their government. In short, failed states create conditions that are ripe for violence. This is especially true when serious ethnic, religious, or economic tensions already exist within the society.

In addition to Sierra Leone, other examples of failed states in Africa include Congo/Zaire after the collapse of the Mobutu regime, Liberia after the overthrow of the despotic Doe government, and Somalia after the end of the Siad Barre era. In each of these cases, the country descended into civil war and ethnic violence, as various factions led by warlords struggled for power. In each case, the civil war can be blamed in large measure on the decades of authoritarian rule that led to state failure.

Authoritarian governments may hold on to power for a long time by cracking down on opposition groups and exploiting ethnic differences within the country. All too often, however, the fault lines of despotic and authoritarian governments crack open. Frequently, the result is civil war.

4 ETHNICITY AND CIVIL WAR

Because Africa's civil wars are frequently fought along ethnic lines, some people have assumed that these wars are caused by ethnic conflict or historical animosity among Africa's many ethnic groups. However, ethnic differences alone do not usually cause civil war. Instead, other factors—such as the struggle for political power, economic disparity, the location of natural resources, and religion—tend to exacerbate tensions between ethnic groups. It is the combination of these factors that often cause conflict; ethnic tensions merely become complicating factors that may even be purposefully exploited by one or more sides to the conflict.

Some scholars believe that extremely diverse societies make civil war less likely. If no single ethnic group is able to dominate the others, they theorize, all groups must find a way to live together. This may help to explain why some of Africa's most ethnically diverse nations—such as Gambia, Ghana, Kenya, Mali, and Senegal—

have never experienced serious ethnic-related violence, while relatively homogenous societies such as Algeria have experienced devastating civil wars. These scholars claim that highly polarized societies—in which one dominant group exerts control over one or more minority ethnic groups—are more likely to experience domestic conflict and violence.

This is not to overlook the fact that Africa's civil wars often have witnessed savage ethnic-related violence, and that the competing armies in African civil wars are frequently based on ethnic allegiance. Once fighting breaks out, civilians tend to gravitate to fellow members of their ethnic group for reasons of safety and security.

CASE STUDY: BURUNDI

Unlike the principal states of Europe, which evolved along distinct ethnic lines, most modern African states are artificial creations of the former colonial powers. European powers partitioned their African holdings into states with little regard for the location of various ethnic groups. Moreover, the colonial powers often manipulated, and even encouraged, ethnic animosity among the different groups under their control as a means of preventing the formation of a nationalist anti-colonial opposition movement. Ethnic groups that were more cooperative with the colonial powers benefited economically, thus creating economic disparities between ethnic groups that continued after independence.

Politically driven conflicts that developed along ethnic lines occurred in the central African states of Rwanda and Burundi during the mid-1990s. In both countries, the Hutu people make up more than 80 percent of the population, while the Tutsi ethnic group makes up around 15 percent. However, for hundreds of years the Tutsi were politically and economically dominant, controlling most of the wealth and resources. The period of colonial occupation of the region (first by Germany, and later Belgium) worsened tensions between the two ethnic groups. The colonial powers (particularly the Belgians) favored the minority Tutsis, giving them important positions in the colonial government and ensuring their continued dominance over the Hutu majority. Both Rwanda and Burundi achieved independence in 1962, but this did not ease ethnic tensions.

The Tutsi remained in power in Burundi, which was ruled by Mwami (king) Mwambutsa IV. Although the king was a Tutsi, he did appoint some Hutu to government positions. However, the Hutu felt they deserved a greater role in the country's government. Unrest led to several Hutu coup attempts in the 1960s.

The ethnic Tutsi king of Burundi, Mwami Mwambutsa IV, was a moderate ruler who offered government positions to Hutu as well as Tutsi. He was overthrown in a military coup in 1966.

Ultimately, the king was forced from power, and a Tutsi-dominated military dictatorship was formed to replace him in 1966.

Under dictator Michel Micombero, the military intimidated and harassed Hutu, preventing them from participating in government or military service or attending schools. In April 1972, Hutu rebels tried to overthrow the government. Thousands of Tutsi were killed, and the military responded by massacring some 150,000 Hutu. Over the next two decades, Tutsi military dictators continued to rule Burundi, and periodic Hutu rebellions and the military responses to them claimed thousands of lives on both sides.

After a 1988 rebellion in which an estimated 20,000 Hutu were killed, pressure from foreign countries forced Burundi's dictator, Pierre Buyoya, to implement reforms. He permitted democratic elections for president and a legislature in June 1993. In that election, the main Hutu party Front for Democracy in Burundi (FROBEDU) won a majority of seats in the national assembly, and a Hutu named Melchior Ndadaye was elected president.

When a group of disgruntled Tutsi soldiers assassinated Ndadaye in an attempted coup in October 1993, the Hutu responded by attacking and slaughtering Tutsi civilians. The Tutsi-domi-

The Hutu political leader Melchior Ndadaye was the first member of his ethnic group elected president of Burundi. Ndadaye was assassinated in October 1993, during an attempted coup by Tutsi army officers; his death sparked a long-running civil war.

nated military moved to protect the Tutsi, then to avenge their slaughter. Approximately 200,000 people died and another 1.3 million became refugees during the resulting civil war. Fighting did not end completely even after a cease-fire was signed by the government and the main Hutu rebel groups in 2003.

CASE STUDY: RWANDA

An even more devastating civil war occurred in Rwanda; although it did not last as long, larger numbers of Rwandans were killed or displaced. Unlike Burundi, in Rwanda the Hutu had gained control of the government after their country became independent in 1962. The Hutu used violence against the Tutsi minority to maintain control during the 1960s, 1970s, and

Rwandan Hutu civilians flee from the Tutsi-dominated military in northern Burundi, March 1995. Ethnic differences are a common contributor to civil wars, and during the 1990s led to genocidal fighting between Hutu and Tutsi in Rwanda and Burundi.

1980s. This bred a vicious cycle of violence: Tutsi who fled to neighboring countries organized attempts to overthrow the Rwandan government; when these failed, the government ordered deadly reprisals against Rwandan Tutsi in which tens of thousands were killed and more Tutsis fled from their homes.

In 1990, the Hutu-Tutsi violence reached a new dimension as a Tutsi-dominated group calling itself the Rwandan Armed Forces (in French, Force Armée Rwandais, or FAR) invaded Rwanda from bases in southern Uganda. FAR fought a guerrilla war against government troops; in addition to fighting the rebels, government forces attacked Rwandan Tutsis, which it argued were supporting the Rwandan Armed Forces. Government radio stations broadcast anti-Tutsi propaganda, claiming that the Tutsi invaders wanted to enslave the Hutu. In addition, some Hutu officials of the Rwandan government began secretly forming armed militias called *interehamwe* ("coming together").

During 1992, peace talks aimed at bringing the two sides together made moderate progress, and on January 10, 1993, the government and opposition parties signed the Arusha Accords. This agreement would open the way to shared power among Hutu and Tutsi parties in Rwanda. To prevent continued Hutu-Tutsi violence, the United Nations sent a peacekeeping force to Rwanda in October 1993.

On April 6, 1994, Rwandan president Juvénal Habyarimana was killed when his airplane was shot down near Kigali airport. No one is certain who was responsible for the assassination— possibly either Hutu extremists or Tutsi rebels—but within an hour of the crash the *interehamwe* militias were attacking Tutsis and moderate Hutus around Kigali. Soon, the violence spread all over the country. Organized gangs roamed through streets hacking Tutsis to death with machetes. More than half of the Hutu population took part in the slayings; the vastly outnumbered U.N. peacekeeping force was unable to protect the Tutsi, and was soon withdrawn. Within 100 days, an estimated 800,000 Rwandans had been slaughtered.

The worst of the fighting ended in July 1994, when the Rwandan Patriotic Force, a Tutsi guerilla army, ousted the Hutu government and established a new Tutsi-dominated government. About 2 million Hutus fled to neighboring Congo. Fighting continued in Rwanda throughout the 1990s. Massive international aid helped to rebuild the shattered economy and resettle refugees, but the challenges were overwhelming. In 2003, Rwanda held peaceful elections for president and the legislature, but ethnic tensions remain high.

Clearly, ethnic differences were a key element of the civil wars in Rwanda and Burundi. But it would be inaccurate to say that they were the root cause of the wars. Instead, both of these

A Rwandan soldier watches as bodies are exhumed from a mass grave near Kibeho. During 100 days in 1994, Hutu extremists massacred an estimated 800,000 Tutsi and moderate Hutu in Rwanda. Western countries and the United Nations failed to respond to the genocide; the fighting eventually ended after a Tutsi rebel group based in Uganda overthrew Rwanda's Hutu-dominated government.

Members of the International Criminal Tribunal for Rwanda are photographed in Arusha, Tanzania. These judges hear cases related to the 1994 Rwandan genocide.

conflicts were over power—in both Rwanda and Burundi, members of one ethnic group controlled the country, and used their power to abuse members of the other group.

MANIPULATING ETHNICITY FOR POLITICAL PURPOSES

Authoritarian leaders have sometimes encouraged and stoked ethnic conflict as part of their strategy for controlling the country—another tactic they learned from their former colonial rulers. Rebel leaders and warlords have also sought to manipulate ethnic passions to advance their own political causes.

In Liberia, for example, rebel leader Charles Taylor launched a guerilla war in 1989 against the country's president, Samuel K. Doe, who himself had come to power through a military coup. Taylor got most of his initial support from among members of his own ethnic group—Americo-Liberians, the descendants of freed

In 1989, Charles Taylor's rebel group started a war to overthrow the government of Liberia. In 2003, Taylor was indicted by a U.N. tribunal for war crimes stemming from violence in Liberia and from his involvement in the Sierra Leonean civil war.

American slaves who had established the country in 1847. Before long, the uprising took on the nature of ethnic warfare, as Taylor's forces targeted members of President Doe's ethnic group, the Krahn, and an allied group, the Mandingoes. Taylor and one of his allies—Prince Johnson—succeeded in overthrowing Doe in 1990, but soon afterward Johnson broke with Taylor's group to form his own militia, supported by the Gio and Mano ethnic groups. Thus, within months, a country in which the various ethnic groups had lived peacefully together found itself embroiled in a three-way civil war that was characterized by ethnic massacres and brutal attacks on civilians. By 1996, an estimated 200,000 Liberians had been killed.

Taylor was elected president of Liberia in 1996, but immediately faced challenges from rival leaders in the north and south of the country. By 2003, Taylor controlled less than one-third of Liberia. Also in 2003, a UN tribunal issued an arrest warrant for Taylor, accusing him of committing war crimes during the civil war.

Under international pressure, Taylor agreed to resign as president and was granted exile in neighboring Nigeria. A UN peace-keeping force was deployed to Liberia to maintain order, but is effectively limited to the area around the capital city of Monrovia; most of the country is under the control of various militia groups. In November 2005, Liberia held relatively peaceful democratic elections. Ellen Johnson-Sirleaf, an economist educated at Harvard, was elected president, becoming Africa's first elected woman president. In April 2006, Charles Taylor was arrested trying to flee Nigeria into neighboring Cameroon. A UN-backed war crimes court plans to try him for his role in atrocities committed during neighboring Sierra Leone's civil war.

As Liberia tries to rebuild and recover, it is deeply scarred by the ethnic hatreds that were fueled by warlords and rebels who sought to manipulate ethnic differences for their own advantage.

The 1996 presidential election in Liberia was generally considered "free and fair." However, as this photo taken outside a polling place indicates, Taylor and his supporters did not hesitate to intimidate voters. Most international observers agree that Liberians voted for Taylor despite his history of violence, because they hoped his election would end the long civil war in their country.

THE SPREAD OF VIOLENCE
DUE TO ETHNIC TIES

One of the characteristics of ethnic conflict in Africa is the "contagion effect"—the tendency for ethnic conflict in one nation to spread to neighboring countries. As already noted, many of Africa's ethnic groups live across national boundaries. As a result, if a particular ethnic group is under attack in one country, members of that group in a neighboring country will become alarmed and seek to provide help. This, in turn, may serve to destabilize the neighboring country.

For example, the flood of Rwandan Hutu refugees into the Democratic Republic of the Congo inflamed tensions in that country, which has a large Tutsi population. In 1996, armed Tutsi militias in Congo started attacking the Rwandan Hutu refugees. (The head of one of the most violent Tutsi militia groups, Laurent Kabila, would later become the key warlord in Congo's civil war.) Facing brutal attacks from these Tutsi militias, around 500,000 Hutu refugees in Congo had no choice but to try and return home to Rwanda, which they had initially fled due to violence. Their return sparked yet more fighting between Tutsis and Hutus, and more deaths.

Similarly, the civil war in Liberia involved ethnic groups and rebel armies that moved freely across Liberia's borders with Sierra Leone, Guinea, and Côte d'Ivoire, destabilizing all three countries. Sierra Leone and Côte d'Ivoire each experienced civil wars of their own, while Guinea, controlled by strongman Lansana Conté, is in danger of becoming a failed state.

5 RELIGION AND CIVIL WAR

istorically, religious differences have been a key element of many conflicts. In Europe, Protestants and Roman Catholics fought numerous religious wars during the 16th and 17th centuries. More recently, conflict has occurred between Catholics and Protestants in Northern Ireland, Christians and Muslims in Lebanon, Muslims and Hindus in India, and Hindus and Buddhists in Sri Lanka.

In Africa, religious conflict is a relatively recent phenomenon. Prior to the arrival of Europeans, most of the people of sub-Saharan Africa practiced various animist religions, which generally involved a belief in spirits and deities that inhabit natural objects such as trees or rivers. African ethnic or tribal groups might have gone to war over territory or resources, but religious differences were rarely the basis for intertribal conflict.

This began to change with the spread of two of the world's major religions, Christianity and Islam, into sub-Saharan Africa. Christianity

(Opposite) A French missionary is surrounded by Christian children in Belgian Congo, circa 1958. The European colonial powers encouraged missionaries to work among Africans during the 19th and 20th centuries.

62

arrived first—North Africa was part of the Roman Empire when Christianity became the de facto state religion in the fourth century. In fact, one of the most important theologians of the early Church, St. Augustine of Hippo, was a Roman citizen of North Africa. By the early eighth century, however, Islam had supplanted Christianity as the dominant faith in North Africa.

Gradually, Muslim beliefs and practices spread into East Africa, primarily because of Indian Ocean trade among Arabs and Africans, and because of the activities of Muslim missionaries. But Africans often practiced Islam in a syncretistic fashion, incorporating the beliefs and rituals of their older animist religions with Islamic practices.

During the 19th century, at the behest of the colonial powers, Christian missionaries attempted to spread their religion into sub-Saharan Africa. But as with Islam, many Africans combined older rituals with Christian worship. In addition, most Africans

remained tolerant of other belief systems. As a result, religion rarely played a role in Africa's various independence struggles against colonial powers.

After the independence period, however, religion became a more divisive issue in some countries. As with the issue of ethnic conflict, religion was sometimes used by authoritarian leaders to create a wedge between various groups in order to better maintain control. Frequently, such leaders would favor their own religious community at the expense of others, thereby alienating other communities and creating resentment and tension.

In several African states, religion has been a major factor in the civil war. In Algeria, the 1992–2002 civil war was an aspect of the larger global struggle taking place within Islam between those who believed religious laws and beliefs should be the basis of government and everyday life (known as fundamentalists or Islamists) and those who preferred a more secular approach to government. In the civil wars in Nigeria (1967–1970) and Sudan (1983–2003), Christian-Muslim animosity exacerbated tensions related to political and economic disparity among ethnic or regional groups.

CASE STUDY: RELIGIOUS FUNDAMENTALISM IN ALGERIA

After a brutal eight-year-long war in which nearly a million Algerians died, Algeria achieved independence from France in 1962. For the next 30 years, a single political party, the National Liberation Front (Front de Libération Nationale, or FLN), controlled Algeria. By the late 1980s, however, many Algerians were frustrated with FLN's heavy-handed rule. Most people were poor, despite the fact that Algeria controls great resources of oil and natural gas. In 1989, the citizens of Algeria approved a new constitution that called for free and open multiparty elections.

Approximately 100,000 Algerians died during that country's civil war, which lasted from 1992 to 2002.

Algeria is a predominantly Muslim nation—by law, the president is required to be Muslim—but the FLN had governed as a secular, socialist party. Under the new constitution, the FLN's principal opposition came from a religious party called the Islamic Salvation Front (Front Islamique du Salut, or FIS). Leaders of this party expressed a variety of goals, from the moderate to the extreme; however, the main goal of the FIS was to establish an Islamic state, with a theocratic government and laws that are compatible with *Sharia*, or Islamic law.

In the country's first multiparty parliamentary election, in 1991, the Islamic Salvation Front stunned the FLN by winning a majority of seats in the new parliament. Almost immediately, the Algerian military (which was controlled by the FLN) seized control of the government, declared the elections to be void, and banned the FIS.

Algeria quickly descended into civil war between armed FIS militias and the Algerian army. More radical and violent groups, such as the Armed Islamic Group (Group Islamique Armé, or GIA), joined with the FIS and attempted to destabilize the military government and establish an Islamic fundamentalist state by committing terrorist attacks in Algeria's cities and conducting massacres in the countryside. The government-controlled military matched their brutality, killing thousands of Algerians—mostly civilians—in an effort to destroy the Islamist movement.

The FIS and its allies received support from fundamentalist movements throughout the Islamic world and from states such as Iran, where the Islamist government supported the FIS goal of establishing an Islamic state in North Africa. However, in the

Ali Belhadj, a leader of Algeria's Islamic Salvation Front, greets supporters after being released from prison in 2003. Belhadj had been jailed in 1992, when the Algerian government, after a military coup, outlawed the FIS and invalidated the results of 1991 elections.

mid-1990s a split developed among the Islamic parties, and the Armed Islamic Group turned on the Islamic Salvation Front's militia, the Islamic Salvation Army.

The war gradually ended after Algerians returned to the polls in the late 1990s to vote on a new constitution and new parliament. Although the Islamic groups boycotted the elections and declared them to be fraudulent, the new government elected in 1999 appeared to have general popular support. The FIS disbanded its armed militia in 2000, and many combatants accepted the terms of a new amnesty program. The GIA had been practically destroyed by 2002; however, occasionally violence still erupts between the Algerian army and more radical Islamic groups. Approximately 100,000 Algerians died during the civil war, and the country's economy and society were shattered.

CASE STUDY: MUSLIM-CHRISTIAN TENSIONS IN NIGERIA

Nigeria's civil war, which lasted from 1967 to 1970, was one of the first civil wars in post-independence Africa, and also one of the bloodiest. It is estimated that over one million people died from fighting, disease, or starvation. While the conflict had multiple factors (as is the case with all civil wars), religious tensions between the country's Muslims and Christians played an important role.

Of the nearly 300 ethnic groups living in Nigeria, the largest are the Muslim Hausa, who live mostly in the north; the Yoruba, who live in the southwest and are both Christian and Muslim; and the predominantly Christian Igbo, who live in the southeast. From 1960 to 1965, an Igbo-Hausa alliance ruled the country at the expense of the Yoruba. In 1965, however, a new Yoruba political movement formed an alliance with fellow Muslim Hausa in the north, and won a majority in national elections that year.

Fearing marginalization of their ethnic group, Igbo officers in the military overthrew Nigeria's government in January 1966. However, a counter coup by the northerners in July 1966 forced the Igbo from power. The Igbo living in the northern part of the country were victims of massacres at the hands of Muslims. In response, the Igbo in the south declared their independence as a new Christian majority nation, the Republic of Biafra.

Because much of Nigeria's oil reserves were in the southern areas claimed by Biafra, the Nigerian government immediately responded to the declaration of secession by invading Biafra and imposing a land and sea blockade on the area.

The Nigerian blockade and military assault succeeded in crushing the state of Biafra, and by 1970 the war was over and Nigeria reunified. But the brutal nature of the blockade—which led to mass starvation and disease—attracted the sympathy of the world, and the Nigerian government was accused of gross human rights abuses.

CONTINUING TENSION IN NIGERIA

The end of the civil war did not eliminate religious and ethnic tensions in Nigeria. During the 1970s and 1980s, the military continued to have a strong influence over government, and power changed hands several times through coups. Although the country returned to civilian rule in 1999, hundreds of people are still killed each year in clashes between Muslims and Christians.

One factor that has contributed to the tension is the implementation of *Sharia* courts in 12 of Nigeria's northern provinces, where large numbers of Muslims live. These courts apply strict penalties to those who transgress against Islamic law; for example, the hands of thieves are cut off. Supporters of the courts say the harsh penalties help reduce crime, but many non-Muslims feel that the laws are outdated and unfair, and some Christians feel they create an atmosphere of intimidation.

In 2004, for example, more than 1,000 people were killed in fighting between Christians and Muslims. More riots broke out in early 2006, when angry Nigerian Muslims used the publication of cartoons considered offensive to Islam as an excuse to riot in several northern cities, attacking and killing Christians and burning churches. In the south, Nigerian Christians responded by burning mosques and Muslim-owned shops and killing Muslims.

It is important to keep in mind, however, that at the core, the Muslim-Christian tension in Nigeria is not about religious differences. Instead, religion provides a convenient dividing

Nigerians walk past a mosque damaged during riots in Onitsha, February 2006. Hundreds of Nigerians are killed each year in violence between Christians and Muslims.

line between populations that differ ethnically, culturally, and—perhaps most important—economically. "Recent violence may have been caused as much by economic envy as religious disputes," noted a *BBC News* analysis after riots broke out in the Nigerian city of Kano in October 2001. "Thousands of young [Muslims] have no jobs and no education, and frustrations over economic hardship leave them prey to political opportunists who want to foment violence."

CASE STUDY: THE SUDANESE CIVIL WAR

Sudan, Africa's second-largest country in terms of land area, has been torn by civil war for nearly all of its existence as an independent nation. Northern Sudan is predominantly Muslim in

John Danforth, representing the United States on the U.N. Security Council, shakes hands with Yaya Hussein Babikar of the Sudanese government. To the left is SPLA representative Nhial Deng Nhial. In 2005 a peace agreement officially ended the long-running civil war in Sudan, although tensions still exist and periodic episodes of violence have occurred.

THE AMAZING STORY OF EMMANUEL JAL

By the time Emmanuel Jal was eight years old, he had been conscripted into the rebel Sudan People's Liberation Army (SPLA). Along with hundreds of other young boys, Emmanuel carried a gun and engaged in bloody battles against Sudanese government troops. One of the tasks of the child soldiers was to run through minefields shooting at the enemy; because the children weighed less than adult soldiers, there was less chance that they would set off the mines.

When he was 13, Emmanuel and about 400 other boys deserted the SPLA and began walking to a refugee camp in Ethiopia. The trip was long and hard—Emmanuel nearly starved to death, and at one point contemplated suicide. Only 12 of the boys survived the ordeal.

A British woman who was helping Sudanese refugees adopted Emmanuel. Moved by his story, she smuggled him onto an airplane to Nairobi, Kenya, by stuffing him inside a large suitcase. In Nairobi, Emmanuel was able to attend school and live a relatively peaceful life. He also developed an interest in music, and started composing and singing rap songs. Eventually, a music studio in Nairobi offered to record his music.

Many of Emmanuel's song lyrics were inspired by his experiences as a child soldier, although he advocates religious tolerance and brotherhood. Emmanuel once told an interviewer that music has "helped heal my soul." In 2004, his single "Peace" became a big hit on radio stations in Kenya. In addition to performing and recording, Emmanuel has become a global spokesperson for the Coalition to Stop the Use of Child Soldiers.

religion and Arab in ethnicity. Southern Sudan is non-Arab and non-Muslim; the people who live in the south are ethnically more closely related to African groups in Kenya and Tanzania, and practice either Christianity or traditional African animist religions. However, although religious differences have played a part in Sudan's history of civil war, many other factors have contributed to unrest in the country. The struggle for economic resources is a major factor: oil, one of Sudan's most valuable natural commodities, is located in the South, along with the country's most fertile agricultural lands.

A Muslim member of the Justice and Equality Movement rebel group in Darfur says afternoon prayers before heading out on a patrol. Unlike the long-running Sudanese civil war between the north and the south, the conflict in Darfur has more to do with ethnic and cultural differences than religion. Both sides in the Darfur fighting are predominantly Muslim.

On gaining independence from Great Britain in 1956, a predominantly Arab and Muslim government was formed in Khartoum. The new government immediately faced an insurgency from the Christian South that lasted until 1972 and led to over 500,000 deaths. The accord that ended that civil war broke down in 1983, when the northern-dominated government attempted to establish *Sharia* as the basis for Sudan's national laws. Christians in the South who did not want to be subject to Islamic law launched a second war. This conflict between the government and the Sudanese People's Liberation Army (SPLA) raged for over 20 years. Millions of Sudanese were killed in the fighting, or because of starvation and disease; millions more became homeless refugees.

A feeling of exhaustion among the Sudanese people, along with pressure from the international community, led to a cease-fire in 2003. A peace agreement between the government and the SPLA was signed in January 2005. Under the terms of the agreement, southern Sudan will be autonomous for a period of six years, at which time the people of the south would be allowed to vote on their independence. During the six-year autonomous period, oil revenues from the south's oil fields would be split 50-50 between the southerners and the government in Khartoum. While the agreement has brought an end to the worst of the fighting, many analysts are skeptical about its long-term prospects for success.

While the North-South fighting has subsided, a new conflict has emerged in a region of western Sudan known as Darfur. However, the causes of this conflict are primarily ethnicity, politics, and economics, rather than religious differences. The two sides—Arabs and non-Arabs—fighting in Darfur are both predominantly Muslim.

IDEOLOGY AND CIVIL WAR

Following independence, many of Africa's new states became strategic battlegrounds in the Cold War. This was a period between 1945 and 1991 when the world's two superpowers, the United States and the Soviet Union, struggled for military, economic, and ideological dominance. Although the two nations did not become involved in direct warfare—hence the name "cold war"—they often became involved in proxy wars.

Leaders in both the United States and Soviet Union believed they were in a struggle for the "hearts and minds" of people throughout the world, and they each sought allies on every continent. During the 1960s, at the height of the Cold War, the competition for allies among the new states of Africa was intensified by the fact that many of these states controlled valuable and strategic natural resources, such as oil, uranium, and bauxite (used to manufacture aluminum, an important component in both military and civilian applications). The two superpowers supported their allies by providing financial aid and military weapons; billions of dollars worth of military weaponry flowed to Africa during the Cold War years. If one superpower supported a particular African government, the other superpower often supported guerilla groups that were opposed to that government, and provided the guerillas with weapons and training. Both superpowers had extensive networks of military advisors and intelligence officers throughout Africa.

CASE STUDY: CONFLICT IN ANGOLA

The long and bloody civil war in Angola is a tragic example of a superpower proxy war. Angola was a Portuguese colony for nearly 400 years. Unlike other European colonial powers, Portgual tried to hold onto its African colonies long after most of the continent had achieved independence. Beginning in 1960, Angolans fought a war for independence from Portugal that claimed tens of thousands of lives.

Two principal Angolan independence groups emerged as the leaders of the anti-colonial struggle against Portugal. The Popular Movement for the Liberation of Angola (MPLA), whose base of support was the Kimbundu ethnic group, had close ties to Communist parties in Europe. It was led by António Agostinho Neto, a physician and poet who had been imprisoned by the Portuguese for anti-colonial activities. The other group, the National Union for the Total Independence of Angola (UNITA), was started by Jonas Savimbi, who had studied medicine in Portugal and received a Ph.D. in political science from a university in Switzerland. UNITA was based in the central part of Angola and received most of its support from the Ovimbundo ethnic group. Although the two organizations shared a desire to expel the Portuguese and create an independent Angola, they were divided by ethnic differences, opposing ideologies, and the fiercely competing leadership ambitions of Neto and Savimbi.

Portugal finally pulled out of Angola (and its other major African colony, Mozambique) in 1974. For a very brief period, the MPLA and UNITA formed a government of national unity to rule Angola. But within several months, the government collapsed, and fighting between MPLA and UNITA forces became widespread. In November 1975, MPLA troops captured Luanda, the capital, and announced the establishment of the Marxist People's Republic of Angola. Agostinho Neto was declared the country's president. But much of the Angolan countryside was still under the control of UNITA forces.

LAND MINES

One of the most horrible weapons used in the Angolan civil war was land mines. Land mines are explosives that are discreetly placed just underground or in the brush; when an unsuspecting soldier steps on the mine, he is killed or maimed. Many of the victims of land mines in Angola, however, were not soldiers, but civilians—farmers, cattle-herders, refugees fleeing the war, and, all too often, children. Both MPLA and UNITA used land mines extensively. No one knows for sure how many land mines were placed in Angola—estimates range as high as six million.

Because land mines are always armed, much of Angola's territory is still considered extremely dangerous, even though the civil war has officially ended. As refugees attempt to return to their original homes, many inadvertently cross minefields. Thousands of Angolans have lost one or more legs to a land mine, and virtually every day land mines claim another victim.

A number of international organizations have sent deminers to Angola to find and deactivate land mines, but this is a slow, dangerous, and expensive process. The Halo Trust, a British charity founded by a former British army officer, is working in Angola (and other African countries) to remove land mines, using advanced techniques to recognize and deactivate them. Halo officials estimate it may take up to ten years to rid Angola of all its land mines.

The Soviet Union and its communist allies immediately embraced the MPLA government. The Soviet Union supplied military equipment to the MPLA, and encouraged its ally Cuba to send 16,000 soldiers to help the MPLA win its conflict with UNITA. On the other hand, the United States refused to recognize the communist MPLA government, even though a majority of African countries and many others around the world did. In keeping with its foreign policy of preventing the spread of communism, the U.S. began to supply weapons and money to UNITA. Two U.S. allies in Africa, Zaire and South Africa, also came to UNITA's assistance. As a result, the conflict in Angola quickly transformed from a post-independence power struggle between the MPLA and UNITA into a major battlefield of the Cold War.

From 1980 to 1990, the Angolan civil war intensified. With strong support from the anti-communist Reagan administration, UNITA launched attacks against infrastructure targets such as dams, railroads, power stations, and oil pipelines in order to undermine the MPLA government. MPLA and Cuban troops responded by staging attacks against UNITA strongholds. UNITA controlled large areas of territory in the

A young MPLA soldier sits in a doorway under a poster of the Marxist leader António Agostinho Neto. Angola became a key battleground in the Cold War, pitting the Soviet-supported Marxist forces under Neto against Jonas Savimbi's UNITA, which was backed by the West.

An MPLA soldier patrols an oil pipeline, March 1993. UNITA forces targeted the country's infrastructure during the civil war in Angola.

countryside, including some principal diamond-producing areas, but the MPLA controlled most of the cities and the major oil-producing areas. South Africa sent more troops to Angola to help UNITA, and the U.S. Congress provided more financial aid and weaponry. UNITA's leader, Jonas Savimbi, traveled to Washington several times during the 1980s, where the guerilla leader was treated like a visiting head of state. Meanwhile, the Soviet Union continued to arm the MPLA, and even more Cuban troops were sent to Angola, their numbers reaching 50,000 by 1990.

Angola's economy was virtually destroyed by the fighting. UNITA attacks made it almost impossible to transport Angola's oil to market. Farmers fled their fields, entire villages were deserted, and the once self-sufficient country was threatened by famine. By 1990, an estimated 300,000 Angolans had been killed and thousands more wounded, including 20,000 who lost one or more limbs. The country's total economic damage was estimated to be over $12 billion.

In 1988, amidst signs that Cold War tensions were easing, the United States started exploring with all sides the possibility of a negotiated resolution to the civil war, an outcome that the Soviet Union also now favored. The main U.S. interest, however, was an agreement that would remove Cuban troops from Angola. In exchange, the United States would persuade South Africa to grant independence to the country of Namibia. An agreement was reached in December 1988, under which Namibia would become independent in March 1990 and all Cuban troops would be withdrawn from Angola by July 1991.

But although the superpowers could congratulate each other on ending their proxy war, the agreement did not end the civil war between the MPLA and UNITA. The Angolan conflict dragged on for another decade. It was not until Savimbi was killed in a 2002 battle against MPLA forces that Angola truly started to move toward reconciliation. Democratic elections planned for 2006 offer hope for the future.

AUTHORITARIAN RULERS ENCOURAGED

Superpower competition in Africa typically encouraged the rise of "strongmen"—authoritarian leaders who ruled with near total power, based on their control over military and police forces. These African leaders frequently became clients of one of the superpowers. Both the Americans and the Soviets found it easier and more effective to support and prop up a strong leader

The rebel leader Jonas Savimbi used the proceeds from illegally mined diamonds to pay for UNITA's resistance to the Angolan government. Although several peace agreements were signed during the 1990s, the civil war did not truly end until Savimbi was killed in a battle during 2002.

who had total control over his country, rather than allow a more democratic political process to produce a leader who might not support the superpower's interests.

Unfortunately, this policy of the superpowers did not help African countries develop democratic and pluralistic political systems. On the contrary, Africa's strongmen generally suppressed all opposition (using the weapons provided by their superpower patrons) and committed terrible human and civil rights abuses to maintain their hold on power. They relied on members of their own ethnic groups to be their major source of support within the country, and rewarded family members and relatives with positions in government and the military. These practices alienated other ethnic groups and fomented resentment that often led to resistance and violence.

Mobutu Sese Seko was an African strongman who established a one-party state in Zaire and ruled the country as if it were his personal possession—very similar to the way Belgian King Leopold had once ruled Congo. Mobutu demanded total loyalty from his people. His government was characterized by corruption and economic mismanagement. Much of Zaire's wealth was siphoned off into Mobutu's personal bank accounts in Switzerland. While most of the Congolese people lived in abject poverty, Mobutu became a billionaire. Mobutu was a master at playing off one ethnic group against another to keep all of them weak, and he made sure that potential opponents were either paid off or suppressed.

Mobutu allied himself with the United States in the struggle against communism and the Soviet Union. He supported anti-communist rebels in Angola's civil war and allowed U.S. military aid to UNITA to be shipped through Zaire. He also welcomed large U.S. and European companies into Zaire to exploit the country's rich mineral resources. In return, Mobutu's government received hundreds of millions of dollars in economic and military aid from the United States and other Western governments, which he used primarily to prop up his regime.

CHANGING SITUATION, CHANGING SIDES

In one instance, an African leader changed sides during the midst of the Cold War. Mohammed Siad Barre came to power in the East African nation of Somalia via a military coup in 1969. He and his supporters arrested political opponents and created a Supreme Revolutionary Council to run the government. Barre was a Marxist, and declared Somalia to be a socialist state. Somalia received millions of dollars in economic and military aid from the Soviet Union; in return, he gave the Soviet navy access to the important port of Berbera on the Gulf of Aden.

In 1974, a coup in neighboring Ethiopia led to the overthrow of that country's emperor, the pro-Western Haile Selassie. Ethiopia's new leader, Mengistu Haile Miriam, expelled Americans from the country and sought Soviet support. Mengistu also provoked Somalia into a war over a disputed border region. The Soviets were in a bind—two of their African allies were at war. Feeling that Ethiopia was the bigger prize, the Soviet Union supported Mengistu. In retaliation, Barre appealed to the United States for aid, which he received in exchange for expelling the Soviet

Somali president Mohammed Siad Barre, photographed at a 1990 summit of the Arab League. Barre became an American client during the 1970s, but at the end of the Cold War the U.S. withdrew its support. Without the backing of the United States, Barre's government was overthrown in 1991 and Somalia descended into chaos and civil war.

Navy from Berbera and granting port rights there to the U.S. Navy.

When the Cold War came to an end in the early 1990s, both the United States and Russia withdrew much of their support for Africa's strongmen. The superpowers simply did not need their African allies anymore now that their competition for global influence had ended. Without support from their former patrons, some African leaders suddenly found it difficult to maintain control of their countries. Many opposition forces were now emboldened to challenge Africa's strongmen; they knew that the superpowers would no longer come to their aid. The opposition forces, however, were often themselves led by men who were not committed to democracy or the well-being of all the people in their countries. Many were opportunistic warlords whose only interest was in securing power and wealth.

POST-COLD WAR UNREST

It is no coincidence that some of Africa's most violent and long-lasting civil wars began after the Cold War ended. When the superpowers no longer felt the need to prop up allies and maintain a certain degree of order and stability in Africa, hostilities and grievances that had built up over the years bubbled to the surface. Moreover, the proliferation of weapons during the Cold War contributed to a recipe for violence and conflict. The United States alone provided over $1.5 billion worth of weapons to African states between 1950 and 1990. According to the World Policy Institute, Liberia, Somalia, Sudan, and Zaire (known today as the Democratic Republic of Congo) were among the countries that received the most arms from the United States; each of these countries experienced periods of violent instability and civil war after 1990.

In Somalia, for example, Siad Barre was opposed by certain ethnic groups and tribes, and during the late 1980s these rivals began to capture territory in northern Somalia. Barre implemented a harsh crackdown against these opposition groups. According to a 1990 report by Africa Watch, which is affiliated with the international organization Human Rights Watch, between 50,000 and 60,000 Somalians were killed in the fighting between 1988 and 1990. Brutal massacres by Barre's troops turned U.S. opinion against him, and the United States cut off much of its aid in 1990. In 1991, Barre was overthrown.

Soon afterward, a full-fledged civil war broke out among rival groups in Somalia. The northern part of Somalia seceded and created a new state, called the Republic of Somaliland. The rest of the country, including the capital city of Mogadishu, became a battleground between two powerful factions. The war disrupted economic activity and led to mass starvation throughout Somalia. In 1992, the United Nations sent a force of peacekeepers to

During the Cold War, both the United States and Soviet Union supplied weapons and military aid to the authoritarian rulers of many African countries. The easy availability of weapons and military training has contributed to conflict in Africa.

Somalia in an attempt to bring an end to the fighting and the humanitarian crisis it had caused; the UN force included about 30,000 American troops. The UN force was unable to maintain order, and withdrew in 1995. A number of Somali factions agreed to a peace treaty in January 2004, but the secessionist Republic of Somaliland refused to participate.

Today, Somalia is a completely failed state. The country does not have a national leader or effective central government. Even before the 1990s Somalia was one of the world's poorest and least developed countries; today, the government cannot provide even the most basic services to its people. Since 1991, foreign nations and groups such as the UN have attempted national reconciliation more than a dozen times; to date, none have succeeded. Somali factions, often led by regional warlords, regularly fight small wars with each other over territory.

CIVIL WAR IN CONGO

Congo/Zaire also plunged into civil war following the withdrawal of U.S. support in the early 1990s. Even with substantial support from the United States and France, Mobutu always struggled to stay in control of his large, multiethnic nation. Political opponents to Mobutu were quickly silenced, but opposition to his regime simmered under the surface. In the early 1990s, as the Cold War came to an end, Mobutu's usefulness to his former supporters in the United States and France declined. The western nations no longer viewed communism as a global threat, and positive political change was occurring in South Africa and Angola. The United States began to side with those in Congo/Zaire who were calling for democracy, transparency and an end to one-man rule, and reduced the amount of aid supplied to Mobutu's government. Mobutu's opponents in Congo/Zaire were emboldened and started to openly agitate for a change in regime.

The various groups and factions that opposed Mobutu coalesced at the end of 1996 into the Alliance of Democratic Forces for the Liberation of Congo-Zaire (AFDL). The AFDL was headed by Laurent Kabila, a Marxist rebel leader who had long opposed Mobutu, and for the previous 30 years had lived in virtual hiding with a small rebel army in the mountains of southeastern Congo/Zaire; he survived by smuggling gold out of the country, but posed no real threat to Mobutu.

But in late 1996, with assistance from the neighboring country of Rwanda and benefiting from the state of disarray in eastern Congo/Zaire, Kabila started to make military gains. The Zairian Army was no match for the rebels, who advanced throughout early 1997, capturing one town after another. Thousands of government troops defected and joined the AFDL rebels. By spring, Kabila controlled about a quarter of the country, and was meeting little serious resistance. Mobutu recruited foreign mercenary soldiers to try and stop the AFDL assault, but as his army and government collapsed, Mobutu spent most of his time in France, where he was undergoing treatment for cancer and where he maintained a lavish home.

Several attempts to achieve a negotiated solution to the civil war failed, mainly because Kabila saw no need to seek a compromise

Laurent Kabila, a Marxist rebel in Congo, was able to overthrow the corrupt Mobutu government after the U.S. withdrew its support. Since Kabila became president of the Democratic Republic of the Congo in 1997, the country has been torn by a civil war in which millions of people have died.

South African leader Nelson Mandela (center) brokered a meeting between Mobutu and Kabila in May 1997, but the two enemies failed to agree on terms of a cease-fire.

when his rebel army was winning every battle. Eventually, South African President Nelson Mandela succeeded in bringing Mobutu and Kabila together for a meeting in May 1997; Mobutu offered to resign in exchange for a cease-fire, but Kabila refused. His troops were by then on the outskirts of Kinshasa, Congo/Zaire's teeming capital city. Less than two weeks later, Mobutu left the country for Morocco, never to return; he died of cancer four months later. On May 17, 1997, AFDL forces entered Kinshasa and declared the establishment of the Democratic Republic of Congo, with Kabila as president. The civil war had led to the deaths of an estimated four million Congolese. Tragically, Congo/Zaire's suffering was not over. Kabila was soon ruling in an authoritarian manner, and opposition to his government quickly led to a second civil war.

7 RESOLVING AFRICA'S CIVIL WARS

There are no easy explanations for the causes of most African civil wars, and therefore no easy solutions to preventing or resolving these conflicts. Most of the contributing causes of Africa's civil wars—such as extreme poverty and economic disparity, weak governmental institutions, and a lack of real democracy in which all people feel that they have a voice in how their nation is run—are major problems throughout Africa. Successful efforts to address these problems may help to ameliorate the plague of civil war.

Many specific remedies have been suggested as ways to prevent future civil wars in Africa. Among the proposals from experts who study the continent and its problems are: increased economic aid from wealthy countries, restrictions on the flow of weapons to Africa, and active intervention in civil conflicts by peacekeeping troops sent by other nations (such as the United States) or groups (like the African Union, United Nations, or European Union).

INCREASING ECONOMIC AID

African countries have received billions of dollars in economic aid since achieving independence, yet the majority of Africans are still desperately poor. Much of the aid given to African states was spent unwisely, or ended up in the pockets of authoritarian leaders. During the Cold War, economic aid was given by the superpowers for the primary purpose of bolstering allies, and only secondarily for helping the African people. And although Africa has historically benefited from extensive foreign aid, it also has suffered from trade barriers in wealthy countries that keep their markets closed to many of Africa's products. Moreover, many African states have borrowed funds from banks and governments in Europe and the United States, and today

Protestors demonstrate against trade barriers and high debt in Durban, South Africa. Some economists agree with African leaders that debt forgiveness would help African countries build more stable economies. If relief measures could reduce poverty and generally improve peoples' standard of living, one of the chief causes of civil wars in Africa would be eliminated.

owe large debts. In some cases, the amount of foreign aid an African nation receives is less than the amount it must pay annually to service its debt. Many Africans and a number of prominent leaders in the West have called for debt "forgiveness" for African states as a means of helping their economies; the United States and several European nations have already undertaken select "forgiveness" programs.

While economic aid certainly may help address problems such as AIDS, famine, natural disasters and poor infrastructure, more money alone will not prevent conflict in Africa. Aid to African states must be allocated wisely to have the greatest benefit. For example, it is vital that economic aid to African countries be targeted to address inequalities in those societies. This will help to heal the social and ethnic rifts that have frequently contributed to civil war.

Another potentially helpful target of foreign aid would be local private organizations in African countries that are working to alleviate poverty, resolve social conflicts, encourage tolerance, and promote democracy and a more open society. These organizations—which as a group often are referred to as "civil society"—have the potential to transform their nations and pave the way to true democracy. And because they are locally run and staffed, they are in the hands of people who have a real stake in a better future for their countries.

HALTING THE FLOW OF ARMS

Far too many African countries are awash in guns, especially so-called "small arms,"—weapons an individual soldier can carry, such as pistols, assault rifles, automatic weapons, grenades, and mortars. Virtually all of these weapons are imported, most by unscrupulous international arms dealers and manufacturers who supply governments and warlords with weaponry in exchange for diamonds, gold, or cash. These arms dealers have

Experts believe that the preponderance of weapons in Africa—particularly small arms, such as the ones pictured here—helps fuel civil wars.

been known to supply multiple sides in the same conflict—their objective is pure profit.

Some observers have argued that efforts to halt the sale of arms to Africa would bring an end to, or at least a reduction in, civil violence. In theory, this approach seems reasonable: without weapons, there can be no warfare. But in reality, it is hard to envision a mechanism for halting the flow of arms. As long as there are arms dealers with a supply of weapons, and African leaders with access to valuable resources or cash, the two will undoubtedly find a way to do business. Any effort to reduce the flow of arms to regions in conflict will help ease suffering and misery; but this alone is not a realistic solution to Africa's civil wars.

OUTSIDE INTERVENTION IN CIVIL CONFLICTS

One of the greatest tragedies of Africa's civil wars is that they have been allowed to develop and continue before the eyes of the world, with very little effort made by foreigners to intervene. The horrible civil war and associated massacres in Rwanda took place in full view of the world—thanks to modern media communications—and yet were allowed to continue until hundreds of thousands of innocent people were killed. And Rwanda is not a unique case: Civil wars in Angola, Somalia, Congo, Liberia, and Sierra Leone were also widely reported on, but evoked only minimal intervention by outsiders. Often, western nations would send military forces to rescue their own citizens, and then quickly leave the scene.

In light of this poor record of outside assistance, a number of prominent African leaders have started to argue that Africans must themselves work to intervene in the conflicts and crises that plague their continent. In 1991 the President of Nigeria, Olusegun Obasanjo, proposed that the Organization of African Unity (the forerunner of the African Union) establish a permanent Conference on Security, Stability, Development, and Cooperation (CSSDC) in Africa. The CSSDC would create a peacekeeping force, composed of troops from many African states, to intervene in civil conflicts. It would also work to promote conflict prevention by establishing an African Peace Council of elder statesmen to mediate conflicts. South Africa's president Thabo Mbeki has offered similar proposals.

In 2003, Nigeria sent troops to Liberia as part of a multinational African peacekeeping force. This force helped to bring about an end to Liberia's civil war, and could serve as a possible model for future African-led peacekeeping operations. The force later came under the control of the United Nations. Nigeria is Africa's most populous nation, and South Africa enjoys the continent's largest economy. It is therefore encouraging that the presidents of these two nations are taking the lead in addressing one of Africa's most serious problems.

A Nigerian member of the African Union peacekeeping force sent to Darfur in 2004 stands in front of protesting villagers in Nyala, Sudan.

CREATING PEACE THROUGH RECONCILIATION

Intervention to help end a conflict is only part of the solution, however. The task of rebuilding societies that have been devastated by civil wars in order to prevent a resumption of violence—a process known as "peacebuilding"—is equally important. Rebuilding often begins with the terms of the peace agreement or accord that ends the civil war. If that agreement is not carefully drafted, and does not address the various tensions that led to war in the first place, it is unlikely to last. Several African civil wars—including those in Angola, Liberia, and Somalia—were temporarily halted by inadequate agreements that later collapsed, leading to a resumption of violence.

Peacebuilding also includes measures to deal with the economic or political sources of conflict, as well as regional or ethnic tensions that may have contributed to the violence. There may need to be a way to prosecute those guilty of war crimes: if the guilty are not brought to justice, the society will have a hard time healing. This was the case in Rwanda, as the International Criminal Tribunal for Rwanda (ICTR) was established by the U.N. Security Council to prosecute those responsible for the 1994 genocide.

The ICTR, which is based in Arusha, Tanzania, and is composed of 25 prominent judges from 24 different countries, is the first international court ever established to deal with the crime of genocide. The tribunal was established to ensure that perpetrators of genocide and other human rights abuses in Rwanda would be held accountable by the international community. As of 2005, the tribunal has brought charges against 23 individuals, and found 20 of them guilty of crimes related to genocide. Over a dozen more are awaiting trial. Among those who have been brought before the ICTR are a former prime minister of Rwanda, several senior government officials, military commanders, and private citizens who took part in massacres. The tribunal plans to continue investigating the Rwandan genocide until all of those involved have been brought to justice.

REORGANIZING AND IMPROVING GOVERNMENT

In addition, government institutions may need to be restructured in order to better reflect the needs of society. If democratic political systems are implemented, they will help ensure that all groups have a voice in the country's political decisions. Governments need to be made less corrupt and more "transparent"—meaning that governmental decisions should be made in clear view and subject to debate and discussion. Governmental

A South African man waits in line to vote in municipal elections in Cape Town. Civil wars are extremely rare in countries where elections are free and fair, government operates in an open manner, and the rule of law is strictly observed.

transparency is the only way to prevent the kind of authoritarian rule that has enriched despotic leaders while impoverishing entire nations. One way to bring about better transparency is to encourage and support the growth of civil society organizations.

Peacebuilding is a long-term process, and one that is wrought with potential problems. But without aggressive measures to rebuild war-torn societies, the chances of new civil wars breaking out will remain high. Perhaps the best way that wealthy nations can help Africans bring about an end to decades of civil war is by providing assistance to help the peacebuilding process in societies that have been traumatized by war.

Equally important is to identify those nations that have the potential to descend into civil war, based on the various risk factors that are well-known to observers. In these countries, conflict prevention measures are required. This involves steps similar to those necessary in peacebuilding. Especially important is to identify those countries that meet the criteria of "failed states," for these are the nations most at risk of a descent into violence. In 2006, Zimbabwe, Guinea, and Côte d'Ivoire all tottered on the verge of civil conflict.

CONCLUSION

Some of Africa's worst civil wars have ended due to a combination of outside intervention, victory by one of the protagonists, or merely the exhaustion of all parties involved. But this does not mean that the threat of civil wars in Africa has ended. Many of Africa's countries are still vulnerable to the kind of conflict that has plagued the continent, and unless steps are taken—first and foremost by Africans themselves, with the aid and assistance of the rest of the world—it is only a matter of time before another African nation suffers the horrors of civil war. Fortunately, the policies necessary to reduce the chances of civil war do not require vast sums of money. They do, however, require the restructuring of African governments and societies, and the vigilance of concerned leaders throughout the continent and the world.

An end to civil conflict in Africa, and the establishment of democratic governments that reflect the will of their citizens, will open the door to an African renaissance, and a future in which the African people finally are able to benefit from their continent's invaluable natural and human resources.

GLOSSARY

ANIMIST—the belief that natural objects, such as trees, rocks, or rivers, are inhabited by spirits; basis for many traditional African religions.

AUTHORITARIAN—a governmental system in which the leader rules with absolute power and authority.

AUTONOMOUS—independent; not under the control of others.

CAPITAL FLIGHT—a circumstance that occurs when money or valuable assets flow rapidly out of a country, usually due to an economic event that disturbs investors, such as the disruption caused by civil war.

CHARISMATIC—having great personal charm or popular appeal.

COLD WAR—a term used to describe the period between 1945 and 1991, when the United States and Soviet Union struggled for dominance and influence in the world.

COLONIALISM—a policy in which one country directly rules outlying territories and uses their labor and resources to increase its power.

COUP D'ETAT—the sudden overthrow of a government, usually through military force.

DECOLONIALIZATION—the process by which a colony gains its independence from the ruling colonial power.

DESPOT—a ruler who governs with absolute power and in a tyrannical manner.

ECONOMIC DISPARITY—a condition in which certain segments or groups in a society receive greater wealth or economic benefits than others.

EPIDEMIC—a rapidly spreading disease or infection.

FUNDAMENTALIST—a religious viewpoint characterized by absolute belief, and often by intolerance of other religious views.

GENOCIDE—the policy of extermination of an entire national, ethnic, or racial group.

GROSS DOMESTIC PRODUCT (GDP)—a measure of the value of all goods and services produced within a nation in a given year.

HOMOGENOUS—being of a similar kind or type.

IDEOLOGY—a set of ideas or theories about society, economics, or politics.

INDIGENOUS—native to a region or area.

INFRASTRUCTURE—the basic facilities and foundations of an economy or society, such as roads, power plants, and schools.

MERCENARY—a soldier-for-hire, who provides his services to any country that will pay him or her.

PLURALISTIC—characterized by many different viewpoints.

POLARIZED—divided into two or more rigid and opposed camps.

PROXY WAR—a conflict in which two powers use third parties as a supplement or a substitute for fighting each other directly.

GLOSSARY

SECESSION—when a region of a country attempts to break away and form a separate country.

SYNCRETISM—the combination of different systems of philosophical or religious belief or practice.

TRADE BARRIER—taxes, quotas, or other economic policies that place limits on the importation of a certain product into a country.

FURTHER READING

Alephonsian Deng, et. al. *They Poured Fire On Us From The Sky: The True Story of Three Lost Boys from Sudan.* New York: Public Affairs Press, 2005.

Arnold, Guy. *Historical Dictionary of Civil Wars in Africa.* Lanham, Md.: Rowman and Littlefield, 1999.

Berkeley, Bill. *The Graves Are Not Yet Full: Race, Tribe, and Power in the Heart of Africa.* New York: Basic Books, 2002.

Gourevitch, Philip. *We Wish to Inform You That Tomorrow We Will be Killed With Our Families: Stories from Rwanda.* New York: Picador Press, 1999.

Herbst, Jeffrey. *States and Power in Africa.* Princeton, N.J.: Princeton University Press, 2002.

Hochschild, Adam. *King Leopold's Ghost.* New York: Mariner Books, 1999.

Meredith, Martin. *The State of Africa: A History of Fifty Years of Independence.* New York: Public Affairs Press, 2005.

Mills, Greg, and Jeffrey Herbst. *The Future of Africa: A New Order in Sight.* London: International Institute for Strategic Studies, 2004.

Pham, John-Peter. *Liberia: Portrait of a Failed State*. New York: Reed Press, 2004.

Reno, William. *Warlord Politics and African States*. Boulder, Colo.: Lynne Riener Publishers, 1999.

Rotberg, Robert I. *When States Fail: Causes and Consequences*. Princeton, N.J.: Princeton University Press, 2003.

Taisier, Ali, and Robert O. Matthews, *Civil Wars in Africa: Roots and Revolution*. Montreal: McGill-Queens University Press, 1999.

Walter, Barbara F. *Committing to Peace: The Successful Settlement of Civil Wars*. Princeton, N.J.: Princeton University Press, 2002.

Zartman, I. William. *Collapsed States: The Disintegration and Restoration of Legitimate Authority*. Boulder, Colo.: Lynne Rienner Publishers, 1995.

INTERNET RESOURCES

HTTP://ALLAFRICA.COM
A comprehensive site devoted to news and developments across Africa.

HTTP://WWW.CRISISGROUP.ORG
The web site of the International Crisis Group, an organization that reports on and analyzes conflicts around the world.

HTTP://WWW.CHILD-SOLDIERS.ORG
The web site of the Coalition to Stop the Use of Child Soldiers. Other good sources of information on child soldiers include http://www.watchlist.org/ and http://www.warchild.org/

HTTP://WWW.AFRICA-UNION.ORG
The web site of the African Union.

HTTP://WWW.PEACE.CA/AFAROUNDAFRICA.HTM
Site of the African Centres for Peace Education and Training.

HTTP://WWW.COMMISSIONFORAFRICA.ORG
In 2004, British Prime Minister Tony Blair established the Commission for Africa to help develop a blueprint for addressing the continent's many problems; this site contains background information and the Commission's report.

INTERNET RESOURCES

HTTP://WWW.PBS.ORG/WGBH/PAGES/FRONTLINE/SHOWS/EVIL/

Website of a special produced by the PBS program Frontline, titled "The Triumph of Evil," on the 1994 genocide in Rwanda.

HTTP://WWW.HRW.ORG

The website for the international organization Human Rights Watch.

HTTP://WWW.AMNESTY.ORG

Website of the international human-rights organization Amnesty International.

INDEX

Numbers in **bold italic** refer to captions.

PICTURE CREDITS

Front cover: Top Photos (left to right): Chris Hondros/Getty Images; L. Downing/US AID; Tyler Hicks/Liaison/Getty Images; Main Photo: Chip Somodevilla/Getty Images

Back cover: Collage of images created by OTTN Publishing with images provided by US AID

CONTRIBUTORS

PROFESSOR ROBERT I. ROTBERG is Director of the Program on Intrastate Conflict and Conflict Resolution at the Kennedy School, Harvard University, and President of the World Peace Foundation. He is the author of a number of books and articles on Africa, including *A Political History of Tropical Africa* and *Ending Autocracy, Enabling Democracy: The Tribulations of Southern Africa*.

WILLIAM MARK HABEEB is an international consultant and adjunct associate professor of conflict management at Georgetown University's School of Foreign Service. He has counseled governments and businesses on issues related to Africa and the Middle East, and is the author of several books, including *Polity and Society in Contemporary North Africa*.